FAḌL IMĀM AL-KHAYRĀBĀDĪ'S
LADDER TO LOGIC

FAḌL IMĀM AL-KHAYRĀBĀDĪ'S LADDER TO LOGIC

المرقاة في علم المنطق

Al-Mirqāt fī ʿilm al-manṭiq

Faḍl Imām al-Khayrābādī

Translation & notes by
MUSA FURBER

ISBN   978-1-944904-21-0 (paper)

Published by:
Islamosaic
islamosaic.com
publications@islamosaic.com

All praise is to Allah alone, the Lord of the Worlds
And may He send His benedictions upon
our master Muhammad, his Kin
and his Companions
and grant them
peace

TRANSLITERATION KEY

ء   ’ (A distinctive glottal stop made at the bottom of the throat.)

ا   ā, a

ب   b

ت   t

ث   th (Pronounced like the *th* in *think*.)

ج   j

ح   ḥ (A hard *h* sound made at the Adam's apple in the middle of the throat.)

خ   kh (Pronounced like *ch* in Scottish *loch*.)

د   d

ذ   dh (Pronounced like *th* in *this*.)

ر   r (A slightly trilled *r* made behind the upper front teeth.)

ز   z

س   s

ش   sh

ص   ṣ (An emphatic *s* pronounced behind the upper front teeth.)

ض   ḍ (An emphatic *d*-like sound made by pressing the entire tongue against the upper palate.)

ط   ṭ (An emphatic *t* sound produced behind the front teeth.)

ظ   ẓ (An emphatic *th* sound, like the *th* in *this*, made behind the front teeth.)

ع   ‘ (A distinctive Semitic sound made in the middle of the throat and sounding to a Western ear more like a vowel than a consonant.)

غ   gh (A guttural sound made at the top of the throat, resembling the untrilled German and French *r*.)

ف   f

ق   q (A hard *k* sound produced at the back of the palate.)

ك   k

ل   l

م   m

ن   n

ه   h (This sound is like the English *h* but has more body. It is made at the very bottom of the throat and pronounced at the beginning, middle, and ends of words.)

و   ū, u

ي   ī, i, y

ﷺ   A supplication made after mention of the Prophet Muhammad, translated as "May Allah bless him and grant him peace."

CONTENTS

المُحْتَوَيَاتُ

TRANSLATOR'S PREFACE

[مُقَدِّمَةٌ]

In the name of Allah the Most Merciful and Compassionate

This booklet presents an English translation of Faḍl Imām al-Khayrābādī's introduction to the science of logic titled *Al-Mirqāt* – translated here as *The Ladder to Logic* – along with the full Arabic text.

ABOUT THE AUTHOR

The author of our text is Faḍl Imām bin Muḥammad Arshad bin Muḥammad Ṣāliḥ bin ʿAbd al-Wājid bin ʿAbd al-Mājid bin al-Qāḍī Ṣadr al-Dīn al-ʿUmarī al-Ḥanafī, originally al-Harkāmī and later al-Khayrābādī. He was born and raised in Khayrābād, where he studied under Mawlānā ʿAbd al-Wājid al-Khayrābādī. He stood unrivalled among his contemporaries in the art of the balance [i.e. logic] and philosophy, and none of his peers disputed his pre-eminence in these fields. He devoted himself entirely to logic and philosophy, teaching, benefiting others, and composing a number of works. He also served the English administration in Delhi, eventually receiving a pension. He had little familiarity with jurisprudence and hadith. He died in Khayrābād on the fifth of Dhū al-Qaʿdah 1243 AH – though there is disagreement about his death, ranging from 1240–1244 AH/1824–1828 CE. Among his works are *Al-Mirqāt fī al-manṭiq* – the present text – a rigorous primer in logic; *Talkhīṣ al-Shifāʾ*, an abridgement of Ibn Sīnā's *Al-Shifāʾ*; a gloss on Mīr Zāhid's treatise; and a gloss on Mīr Zāhid's Mullā Jalāl.[1]

---

1   ʿAbd al-Ḥayy al-Ḥasanī, *Nuzhat al-khawāṭir wa-bahjat al-masāmiʿ wa-l-nawāẓir*, 8 vols. (Beirut: Dār Ibn Ḥazm, 1420/1999), 7:1063; Muḥammad

ABOUT THE BOOK

ABOUT THE BOOK

The book covers the standard topics of classical Arabic logic in the Avicennan tradition. It opens with an introduction to knowledge, conception, and assent, before treating expressions and their meanings in detail. The first chapter covers propositions – their types, quantities, qualities, and modalities – along with conversion and contradiction. The second chapter covers syllogisms in full: the four figures and their productive moods, the conditions for productivity, composite syllogisms including reductio ad absurdum, and the five crafts of demonstrative, dialectical, rhetorical, poetic, and sophistic reasoning, including an extended treatment of formal and material fallacies. The book closes with supplementary remarks on the nature of the sciences and the Eight Headings of the ancients.

ABOUT THE TRANSLATION

In mid-July of 2023, my thesis advisor Dr Muhammad Ayman al-Akiti requested that I translate an introduction to logic. I had already translated Shaykh Muḥammad Yāsīn al-Fādānī's introduction to logic the previous summer, but something lengthier was needed. I needed to review the subject, so I started considering the options. These options included commentaries for Athīr al-Dīn al-Abharī's (d. 663 AH/1264 CE) *Īsāghūjī* – such as al-Mākūti's (d. 760 AH/1359 CE), al-Fannārī's (834 AH/1432 CE), and Shaykh al-Islām Zakariyā al-Anṣārī's (d. 926 AH/1520 CE); the first portion of Saʿd al-Dīn al-Taftāzānī's (d. 793 AH/1391 CE) *Tahdhīb al-manṭiq wa-l-kalām* with notes from al-Khabīṣī's (d. 854 AH/1450 CE) *Tahdhīb*; or Najm al-Dīn al-Qazwīnī al-Kātibī's (600–675 AH/1203–1276 CE) *Shamsiyyah*. Several individuals pointed me to Faḍl Imām al-Khayrabādī's *Al-Mirqāt*. It soon became clear that this was the one to do. I began work on the translation early September 2023 and, *bi-faḍl-Llāh*, I had a classroom edition available by 28 September 2023, which coincides with 13 Rabiʿ al-Awwal 1445 AH.

Ḥifẓ al-Raḥmān al-Kumayllāʾī, *Al-Budūr al-ḍiyyah fī tarājim al-Ḥanafiyyah*, 23 vols. (Cairo: Dār al-Ṣāliḥ; Dhaka: Maktabat Shaykh al-Islām, 1439/2018), 13:336.

The translation makes use of several editions of the book, including:

1. *Al-Mirqāt*, edited by ʿAbd al-Raḥmān bin Aḥmad Āl ʿAbd al-Qādir (n.p.: n.p., c. 1428).
2. *Al-Mirqāt* with *Al-Mirʾāh* by Shaykh Muḥammad ʿImmād al-Dīn al-Shīrkūtī (Karachi: Maktabat al-Bushrā, 1433/2011) – 116 pages. ("al-Bushrā edition" in the footnotes) This edition is cross-referenced in the Arabic text as ‹ب›.
3. *Al-Mirqāt* with *Al-Mishkāt* (Karachi: Maktabah al-Madīnah, 1436/2015) – 104 pages. ("al-Madīnah edition" in the footnotes) This edition is cross-referenced in the Arabic text as ‹م›.
4. *Sharḥ al-mirqāt* by Muḥammad ʿAbd al-Ḥaqq bin Faḍl Ḥaqq al-ʿUmarī al-Khayrābādī, edited by ʿAbd al-Ḥamīd al-Turkmānī (ʿAmmān: Dār al-Nūr, 2019) – 789 pages.
5. *Al-Mirqāt* with Shaykh Muḥammad ʿAbd al-Ḥakīm Sharaf al-Qādūrī's (d. 1428 AH) *Al-Mishkāt*. (Bareilly, Uttar Pradesh, India: Dār al-Malik, 1444/2022) – 224 pages. This edition is cross-referenced in the Arabic text as ‹د›.

Just like the Arabic original, this translation is directed at *ṭullāb al-ʿilm* who will be reading the text with an instructor or already know enough Arabic to access its commentaries and other works on the subject. While the translation aims to make the Arabic original accessible to English readers, translation choices often favour bilingual reading over monolingual reading.

I have added section titles throughout to aid navigation. These supplied titles are distinguished from the author's own by the use of square brackets.

✳ ✳ ✳

Many thanks are owed to the individuals who reviewed drafts of the translation and offered corrections, encouragement, and advice – including Dr Ayman for setting me on this path; SZ and NJ for recommending it; YAK for ongoing exchanges about the text and the genre in general; and MAN, AbAB, QM, and Shaykh HWM for their help with the Persian. Above all, I owe much to my wife and children for their constant support and sacrifices over the years.

May Allah bless the author of the text, those mentioned in the text or footnotes, those who contributed in any way to bringing it to English readers, and their fellow readers. And may He forgive the translator and protect readers from his copious shortcomings.

MUSA FURBER
CYBERJAYA, MALAYSIA
1447 AH/2026 CE

FAḌL IMĀM AL-KHAYRĀBĀDĪ'S LADDER TO LOGIC

المرقاة في علم المنطق

Al-Mirqāt fī ʿilm al-manṭiq

AUTHOR'S INTRODUCTION

[مقدِّمةُ المؤلِّفُ]

بسم اللَّه الرحمن الرحيم

In the name of Allah, the Most Gracious, the Most Merciful

الحمـدُ ‹ب٣› للَّهِ ‹د٣٩› الـذي أبدعَ الأفلاكَ والأرضينَ، والصلاةُ علىٰ مَـن كانَ نبيًّـا وآدمُ بينَ الماءِ والطيـنِ، ‹د٤٠› وعلىٰ آلِه وصحبِه أجمعينَ. وبعدُ:

Praise be to Allah, who created the celestial spheres and the earths. May blessings and peace be upon him who was a prophet while Adam was still between water and clay, and upon his family and all his companions. To proceed:

فهـذهِ ‹د٤١› عـدّةُ فصـولٍ فـي علـمِ الميـزانِ، لا بدَّ مِـن حفظِها وضبطِهـا لمَن أرادَ أنْ يتذكَّرَ مِن أولي الأذهانِ، وعلى اللَّهِ التوكّلُ وهو المستعانُ. ‹ب٤›

These are a few chapters in the science of logic (*'ilm al-mīzān*). They must be memorised and mastered by whoever among those of keen minds wishes to recall [knowledge].[2] Reliance is upon Allah; He is the One whose help is sought.

---

2   (Tr:) The phrase may be understood as referring either to those who wish to be recognised among the foremost intellects or to the foremost intellects themselves who seek to recall and retain knowledge.

1

INTRODUCTORY MATTERS

مقدّمةٌ [في إطلاقاتِ العلمِ ومعنى التصوّرِ والتصديقِ]

مقدّمةٌ اعلمْ أنَّ «العلمَ» يطلقُ ‹د٤٢› على معانٍ.

أحدُها: حصولُ صورةِ الشيءِ في العقلِ. ‹د٤٣›

ثانيها: الصورةُ الحاصلةُ مِن الشيءِ عندَ العقلِ.

ثالثُها: الحاضرُ عندَ المُدرِكِ.

رابعُها: قبولُ النفسِ لتلكَ الصورة. ‹د٤٤›

خامسُها: الإضافةُ الحاصلةُ بينَ العالمِ والمعلومِ. ‹م١، ب٥›

KNOWLEDGE, CONCEPTION, AND ASSENT

Know that *knowledge* (*'ilm*) is applied to various meanings.

The first is the occurrence of a thing's *form* (*ṣūrah*) in the *intellect* (*'aql*).

The second is the form of a thing obtained in the intellect.

The third is that which is present with the perceiver.

The fourth is the soul's reception of that form.

The fifth is the relation that results between the knower and the known.[3]

وهــو ينقسـمُ على قسـمينِ. أحدُهمـا: يُقالُ له: التصـوّرُ. ‹د٤٥›

وثانيهمـا: يُعبَّرُ عنه بالتصديقِ. ‹د٤٦›

---

3   The first four opinions belong to philosophers (*al-ḥukamā'*). The last is the opinion of Muslim theologians (*al-mutakallimūn*). Cf. al-Madīnah edition, 1 fn. 1–3; al-Bushrā edition, 5.

2

It[4] is divided into two parts: one is called *conception* (*taṣaw-wur*), and the other is referred to as *assent* (*taṣdīq*).

أمّا التصوّرُ: فهو الإدراكُ الخالي عن الحكمِ.

As for *conception* (*taṣawwur*), it is *perception* (*idrāk*) devoid of judgement (*ḥukm*).

والمرادُ بالحكمِ: نسبةُ أمرٍ إلى أمرٍ آخرَ إيجابًا أو سـلبًا، وإنْ شئتَ قلتَ: إيقاعًا أو انتزاعًا. وقد يفسَّرُ الحكمُ بوقوعِ النسبةِ أو لا وقوعِها.

What is meant by *judgement* (*ḥukm*) is the relating of one matter to another, affirmatively or negatively. (If you wish, you may say: *positing* (*īqāʿ*) or *removing* (*intizāʿ*).) Judgement may also be explained as the occurrence or non-occurrence of the relation.

كما إذا تصوّرتَ زيدًا وحدَه أو قائمًا وحدَه مِن دونِ أنْ تثبتَ القيامَ لزيدٍ وتسلبَه عنه. (ب٦)

[An example of conception is] such as if you conceptualised *Zaid* alone or *standing* alone without affirming *standing* to *Zaid* or negating it from him.

أمّـا التصديـقُ فهو علىٰ قولِ الحكمـاءِ: عبارةٌ عن الحكمِ المقارِنِ للتصوّراتِ. (د٤٧)، فالتصوّراتُ الثلاثةُ شـرطٌ لوجودِ التصديقِ، ومِن ثَمَّ لا يوجدُ تصديقٌ بلا تصوّرٍ.

As for *assent* (*taṣdīq*), according to the philosophers (*ḥukamāʾ*), it is a judgement that accompanies the conceptions. Thus, the three conceptions[5] are a prerequisite for the existence of assent. Hence, no assent exists without conception.

---

4   Dār al-Malik edition: i.e. knowledge.

5   (Tr:) i.e. *Zaid*, *standing*, and there being a relation between them.

والإمامُ الـرازيُّ يقـولُ: إنَّـه عبارةٌ عـن مجموعِ الحكـمِ وتصوّراتِ الأطرافِ.

Al-Imām al-Rāzī[6] says that assent is the combination of the judgement and the conceptions of the terms.[7]

فإذا قلتَ: «زيدٌ قائمٌ» وأذعنتَ بقيامِ زيدٍ تحصلُ لكَ علومٌ ثلاثةٌ: أحدُهـا: علمُ زيدٍ. وثانيهـا: إدراكُ معنىٰ قائمٍ. وثالثُها: علمُ المعنى الرابـطِ الـذي يُعبَّـرُ عنـه في الفارسيّةِ بـ (هسـت) في الإيجـابِ، وبـ (نيسـت) (م٢) فـي السـلبِ، «ے» و «نهيـن» فـي الهنديّةِ، (ب٧) ويُقالُ هذا المعنىٰ: «الحكمُ» تارةً، و «النسبةُ الحكميّةُ» أخرىٰ.

Thus, when you say, "Zaid is standing," and you assent to Zaid's standing, three items of knowledge arise:

The first is knowledge of Zaid.

The second is perception of the meaning of *standing*.

The third is knowledge of the connective concept (*ma‘nā al-rābiṭ*) expressed in Persian as "هسـت" (hast) for affirmation and "نيست" (nīst) for negation, or in Hindi as "ے" (ha) and "نهين" (nahīn). This meaning is sometimes called *judgement* (ḥukm) and at other times *judgemental relation* (nisbah ḥukmiyyah).

فإذا أتقنـتَ ما علمنـاكَ فاعلمْ أنَّ الحكماءَ يزعمونَ[8] أنَّ التصديقَ (د٤٨) ليـسَ إلّا إدراكَ المعنـى الرابطيِّ، والإمـامَ يزعـمُ أنَّ التصديقَ

---

6   Muḥammad bin ‘Umar bin al-Ḥasan bin al-Ḥusayn, known as "Fakhr al-Dīn al-Rāzī" (543–605 AH / 1148–1209 CE).

7   (Tr:) The two terms of a proposition, i.e. subject and predicate, or antecedent and consequent.

8   Dār al-Mālik and al-Madīnah editions: (الحكماء يزعمون); al-Bushrā edition: (الحكيم يزعم)

مجموعُ الإدراكاتِ الثلاثةِ، أعنـي: تصوّرَ المحكومِ عليـه، وتصوّرَ المحكومِ به، وإدراكَ النسبةِ الحكميّةِ المسمّىٰ بـ «الحكمِ».

If you have mastered what we have taught you, then know that the philosophers claim that assent is nothing but the perception of the connective concept, while al-Imām [al-Rāzī] holds that assent is the combination of the three perceptions, namely: conceptualising the subject, conceptualising the predicate, and perceiving the judgemental relation called *the judgement*.[9]

DIVISIONS OF CONCEPTIONS فصلٌ [في أقسام التصور]

التصوّرُ قسمانِ. أحدُهما: بديهيٌّ، أي حاصلٌ بلا نظرٍ وكسبٍ كتصوّرِنا الحرارةَ ﴿د٤٩﴾ والبرودةَ، ويُقالُ له: الضروريُّ أيضًا. وثانيهما: نظـريٌّ، أي يحتـاجُ فـي حصولِه إلى الفكرِ والنظرِ، كتصوّرِنا الجنَّ والملائكـةَ؛ فإنّـا محتاجونَ في أمثالِ هذهِ التصوّراتِ إلىٰ تجشُّمِ فكرٍ ﴿٣م﴾ وترتيبِ نظرٍ، ويُقالُ له: «الكسبيُّ» أيضًا.

Conception is divided into two parts:
The first is *self-evident* (*badīhī*) – it occurs without discursive reasoning or acquisition, such as our conception of *hot* and *cold*. It is also called *immediate* (*darūrī*).

---

9   In the example "Zaid is standing": *Zaid* is the subject (*mawḍūʿ*), i.e. the recipient of an assertion (*al-maḥkūm ʿalayhi*); *standing* is the predicate (*maḥmūl*), i.e. the assertion received (*al-maḥkūm bihi*); *is* is the relationship being affirmed or negated between the subject and predicate, i.e. the asserted relation (*al-nisbah al-ḥukmiyyah*); whether the relationship is believed to occur or not is the assertion (*al-ḥukm*). Cf. Muḥammad Shams al-Dīn Ibrāhīm Sālim, *Taysīr al-qawāʿid al-manṭiqiyyah* (Karachi: Banūrī, 1422/2001), 9; Quṭb al-Dīn al-Rāzī, *Taḥrīr al-qawāʿid al-manṭiqiyyah* (Qum: Manshūrāt Baydār, 1426/2005), 33–34.

The second is *discursive* (*naẓarī*)[10] – it requires thought and discursive reasoning to occur, such as our conception of *jinn* and *angels*, since for such conceptions, we require undertaking thought and ordering discursive reasoning. It is also called *acquired* (*kasbī*).

DIVISIONS OF ASSENTS   [أقسام التصديق]

والتصديقُ أيضًا قسمانِ. أحدُهما: البديهيُّ الحاصلُ مِن غيرِ فكرٍ وكسبٍ، وثانيهما: النظريُّ المفتقرُ إليـه. ‹د.٥٠› مثالُ الأوّلِ: «الكلُّ أعظـمُ مِن الجزءِ»، و«الاثنانِ نصفُ الأربعةِ». ومثالُ الثاني: «العالَمُ حادثٌ»، و«الصانعُ موجودٌ»، ونحوُ ذلكَ. ‹ب.٨›

Assent is also divided into two parts.

The first is *self-evident* (*badīhī*) – it occurs without thought or acquisition.

The second is *discursive* (*naẓarī*) – it requires them.

An example of the first is: "The whole is greater than the part" and "Two is half of four."

An example of the second is: "The world is originated," "The Maker exists," and similar statements.

BENEFICIAL POINT: DISCURSIVE REASONING   فائدةٌ [النظرِ]

وإذا علمـتَ مـا ذكرنـا أنَّ النظريّـاتِ مطلقًـا - تصوّريّـةً كانـتْ أو تصديقيّـةً - مفتقرةٌ إلـىٰ نظرٍ وفكرٍ فلا بـدَّ لكَ أن تعلمَ معنى النظرِ فأقولُ:

---

10   (Tr:) The translation of these three terms reflects what is found in *Lane's Lexicon* and are used similarly in English language scholastic philosophy and logic books.

When you know what we have mentioned – that discursive matters predicatingly, whether related to conception or assent, depends upon discursive reasoning and thought – then you must understand the meaning of discursive reasoning. I say:

Discursive reasoning (naẓar), in their terminology, is arranging matters which are known in order for that arrangement to result in obtaining an unknown.

فإذا^(١١) رتّبتَ المعلوماتِ (ب٩) الحاصلـةَ لـكَ مِـن تغيّرِ العالَمِ وحدوثِ كلٍّ متغيّرٍ وقلتَ: «العالَمُ متغيّرٌ، وكلُّ متغيّرٍ حادثٌ» فحصلَ لكَ مِن هذا النظرِ والترتيبِ علمُ قضيّةٍ أخرىٰ لم يكنْ حاصلًا لكَ مِن قبلُ وهي: «العالَمُ حادثٌ».

So, if you arrange what you know from the world changing and everything that changes being originated, and say: "The world is changing. Everything that changes is originated," then from this discursive reasoning and arrangement, you will obtain another proposition that had not been available to you before: "The world is originated."

THE NEED FOR LOGIC   فصلٌ [الحاجة إلى المنطق]

إيّاكَ وأنْ تظنَّ أنَّ كلَّ ترتيبٍ يكونُ صوابًا موصِّلًا إلىٰ علمٍ صحيحٍ، كيـفَ ولـو كانَ الأمرُ كذلكَ ما وقعَ الاخـتلافُ والتناقضُ بينَ أربابِ النظرِ مع أنَّه قد وقعَ.

Beware of assuming that every arrangement [of propositions] is correct and leads to sound knowledge. How could that be? If it were so, disagreements and contradictions would not occur among masters of discursive reasoning – yet they have.

---

11   (Tr:) Each is slightly different: (كما إذا), (فإذا), and (إذا).

فَمِـن قائـلٍ (م٤) يقولُ: «العالَمُ حادثٌ»، ويسـتدلُّ بقولِه: «العالَمُ متغيِّرٌ، وكلُّ متغيِّرٍ حادثٌ، فالعالَمُ حادثٌ». (ب١٠، د٥٢)

One person says, "The world is originated," and he argues it by saying "The world is changing. Everything that changes is originated. Thus, the world is originated."

ومِـن زاعِـمٍ يزعمُ أنَّ العالَمَ قديمٌ غيرُ مسـبوقٍ بالعدمِ، ويبرهِنُ عليه بقولِه: «العالَمُ مستغنٍ عن المؤثِّرِ، وكلُّ ما هذا شأنُه فهو قديمٌ».

While another claims that the world is eternal, not preceded by nonexistence, and he proves it by saying: "The world does not depend upon an influencing factor. Everything with this disposition is eternal."

ولا أظنُّكَ شاكًّا في أنَّ أحدَ الفكرينِ صحيحٌ حقٌّ والآخرُ فاسدٌ غلطٌ.

I do not think you doubt that one of these two lines of reasoning is true and correct while the other false and mistaken.

وإذا كانَ قـد وقعَ الغلطُ في فكرِ العقلاءِ فعُلمَ مِن ذلكَ أنَّ الفطرةَ الإنسـانيّةَ غيرُ كافيةٍ في تمييزِ الخطأِ مِن الصوابِ، وامتيازِ القشرِ عن اللبـابِ، فجـاءتْ الحاجةُ في ذلكَ إلىٰ قانـونٍ عاصمٍ عن الخطأِ في الفكـرِ يبيَّـنُ فيه طرقُ اكتسـابِ المجهـولاتِ عن المعلومـاتِ. وهذا القانونُ هو المنطقُ والميزانُ. (ب١١)

Since mistakes occur in the reasoning of intellectuals, it becomes evident that human nature is insufficient for distinguishing between error and correctness and for differentiating the husk from the kernel. Therefore, there arose a need for a law that safeguards against errors in reasoning and clarifies the methods of acquiring what is unknown from the known. This law is *logic (manṭiq)* and *the balance (mīzān)*.

WHY IT IS NAMED "LOGIC"   [وجه التسمية بالمنطق]

أمّا تسميتُه بـ «المنطقِ» فلتأثيرِه في المنطقِ الظاهـريِّ، أعني: التكلّمَ؛ إذْ العـارفُ به يقوّىٰ على التكلّم بما لا يقوّىٰ عليه الجاهلُ، وكـذا فـي النطقِ الباطنيِّ أعنـي: الإدراكُ ‹د٣٥›؛ لأنَّ المنطقيَّ يعرفُ حقائقَ الأشياءِ، ويعلـمُ أجناسَها، وفصولَها، وأنواعَهـا، ولوازمَهـا، وخواصَّها، بخلافِ الغافلِ عن هذا العلمِ الشريفِ.

It is named *logic (manṭiq)* because of its effect upon outward articulation (i.e. speech), as those familiar with it are empowered to speak in ways those ignorant of it cannot. Likewise, [it influences] internal articulation (i.e. perception), since the logician knows the realities of things, their genera, differentia, species, concomitant consequents, and propria – unlike those ignorant of this noble science.

أمّا تسميتُه بـ «الميزانِ» فلأنَّه قسطاسُ للعقلِ تُوزنُ به الأفكارُ ‹م٥› الصحيحةُ، ويُعرفُ به نقصانُ ما في الأفكارِ الفاسدةِ، واختلالُ ما في الأنظارِ الكـاسدةِ، ومِن ثَمَّ يُقالُ له: «العلمُ الآلي»؛ لكونِه آلةً لجميعِ العلومِ، لا سيَّما للعلومِ الحكميّةِ ‹ب١٢›

It is named *the balance (mīzān)* because it is a scale for the intellect, by which correct thoughts are weighed, the deficiencies of flawed thoughts are recognised, and the distortions of corrupt insights are identified. Hence, it is called *the instrumental science (al-'ilm al-ālī)*, as it serves as an instrument for all sciences – especially the philosophical sciences.

BENEFICIAL POINT: ITS FOUNDER فائدةٌ [في واضعِ علمِ المنطقِ]

اعلـمْ أنَّ ارسـطاطاليسَ الحكيـمَ دوَّنَ هـذا العلـمَ بأمرِ الإسـكندرِ الروميِّ وهـذا يلقَّبُ ‹د٤٥›، بـ «المعلَّمُ الأوَّلِ»، والفارابيُّ هذَّبَ هذا الفنَّ، وهو «المعلَّمُ الثاني»، وبعدَ إضاعةِ كتبِ الفارابيِّ فصَّلَه الشيخُ أبو عليٍّ بنِ سينا. (ب١٣)

Know that Aristotle,[12] the philosopher, recorded this science by the order of Alexander the Roman,[13] and he is dubbed the *First Teacher (al-muʿallim al-awwal)*. Al-Fārābī[14] refined this art and is dubbed the *Second Teacher (al-muʿallim al-thānī)*. After the loss of al-Fārābī's books, it was elaborated by Sheikh Abū Alī Ibn Sīnā.[15]

LOGIC DEFINED فصلٌ [في تعريفُ علمِ المنطقِ]

لعلَّكَ علمتَ بما تلونا عليكَ في بيانِ الحاجةِ حدَّ المنطقِ وتعريفَه مِن أنَّه: «علمٌ بقوانينَ تعصمُ مراعاتُها الذهنَ عن الخطأِ في الفكرِ».

Perhaps from what we presented to you in explaining the need for logic, you have learned its definition, namely that *logic (manṭiq)*

---

12 Aristotle, the Ancient Greek philosopher and polymath (384–322BC). His *Prior Analytics* is credited with being the earliest study of formal logic. It, along with his *Categories, On Interpretation, Posterior Analytics, Topics,* and *On Sophistical Refutations* were posthumously compiled into set of six books known as *Organon* (meaning "instrument"). In the Arab world, his *Rhetoric* and *Poetics* were appended to these six.

13 Alexander III of Macedon (356–323BC), commonly known as Alexander the Great. Was a king of the ancient Greek kingdom of Macedon. He was tutored by Aristotle until the age of 16.

14 Abū Naṣr bin Ṭarkhān, of Persian origin (d. 339AH). Was nicknamed "Second Teacher" due his expansive reading of philosophy and his clarifications and commentaries on the writings of Plato and Aristotle.

15 Abū ʿAlī al-Ḥusayn bin ʿAbd Allāh bin Sīnā al-Bukhārī (d. 428 AH/1037 CE).

is a science of laws whose observance safeguards the mind from errors in discursive reasoning.

ITS SUBJECT MATTER

فصلٌ [في موضوعِ علمِ المنطقِ]

موضـوعُ كلِّ علمٍ ﴿٥٥د﴾ مـا يُبحـثُ فيه عن عوارضِـه الذاتيّةِ له، كبـدنِ الإنسانِ للطبِّ، والكلمةِ والكلامِ لعلمِ النحو. فموضوعُ علمِ المنطـقِ: المعلومـاتُ التصوّريّـةُ والتصديقيّـةُ، لكـنْ لا مطلقًا بل مِن حيثُ إنَّها موصِّلةٌ إلى المجهولِ التصوّريِّ أو التصديقيِّ. ﴿م٦، د٥٦﴾

The *subject matter* (*mawḍū'*) of every science is that whose essential properties are examined within it – such as the human body in medicine or words and speech in the science of grammar. Thus, the *subject matter of logic* (*mawḍū' 'ilm al-manṭiq*) is conceptual and judgemental knowledge – but not predicatingly; rather, insofar as it leads to a conceptual or assent-related unknown.

BENEFICIAL POINT: ITS
ULTIMATE GOAL

فائدةٌ [في غايةِ علمِ الميزان]

اعلـمْ أنَّ لـكلِّ علمٍ وصناعةٍ غايـةً، وإلّا لكانَ طلبُه عبثًا والجِدُّ فيه لغوًا. ﴿ب١٤﴾ وغايةُ علمِ الميزانِ الإصابةُ في الفكرِ، وحفظُ الرأيِ عن الخطأِ في النظرِ.

Know that every science and craft has an *ultimate goal* (*ghāyah*), or else its pursuit would be in vain and taking it seriously would be folly. The *ultimate goal of the science of logic* (*ghāyat 'ilm al-mīzān*) is to achieve correctness in thought and to safeguard one's opinion from error in discursive reasoning.

2

INDICATION

فصلٌ [الدلالةُ والألفاظُ]

INDICATION AND EXPRESSIONS

لا شـغلَ للمنطقيِّ مِـن حيثُ إنَّه منطقيٌّ ببحـثِ الألفاظِ، كيفَ وهـذا البحـثُ بمعزلٍ عـن هدفِه وغايتِه. ومع ذلكَ فلا بدَّ مِن بحثِ الألفـاظِ الدالّـةِ على المعاني؛ لأنَّ (د٥٧)، الإفادةَ والاستفادةَ موقوفةٌ عليه، ولذلكَ يقدَّمُ بحثُ الدلالةِ والألفاظِ في كتبِ المنطقِ.

The logician, insofar as he is a logician, has no concern with the investigation of *expressions* (alfāẓ). How could he, when such an investigation is separate from his purpose and goal? However, it is still necessary to investigate expressions that indicate meanings, since communicating and understanding depend on them. For this reason, the study of *indication* (dalālah) and expressions is introduced in books of logic.

فصلٌ: في الدَلالةِ

INDICATION

الدَلالـةُ لغةً هي: الإرشـادُ، أي: «راه نمـودن»، وفي الاصطلاحِ: كونُ الشيءِ بحيثُ يلزمُ مِن العلمِ به العلمُ بشيءٍ آخرَ.

Indication (dalālah), linguistically, means guidance, i.e. to make a path or way.

Technically, it is a thing being such that knowledge of it necessitates knowledge of another thing.

 [أقسامُ الدَّلالةِ]

والدلالةُ قسمانِ: لفظيّةٌ، وغيرُ لفظيّةٍ.

Indication is divided into two parts: verbal and non-verbal.

واللفظيّةُ: (ب١٥) ما يكونُ الدالُّ فيها اللفظَ.

Verbal indication (*lafẓiyyah*) is that in which the expression is the indicator.

وغيرُ اللفظيّةِ: ما لا يكونُ الدالُّ فيها اللفظَ.

Non-verbal indication (*ghayr lafẓiyyah*) is that in which the expression is not the indicator.

وكلٌّ مِنْهما على ثلاثةِ أنحاءٍ.

Each of the two has three varieties.[16]

أحدُها: «اللفظيّةُ الوضعيّةُ» كدلالةِ لفظِ «زيدٌ» على مسمّاهُ. (د٥٨)

The first is *conventional verbal indication* (*lafẓiyyah waḍʿiyyah*) – such as the expression *Zaid* signifying the named person.

وثانيهمـا: اللفظيّـةُ الطبيعيّةُ كدلالةِ لفـظِ «أُحْ أُحْ» - بضمِّ الهمزةِ وسكونِ الحاءِ المهملةِ وقيلَ: بفتحِها - على وجعِ الصدرِ، فإنَّ الطبيعةَ تضطرُّ بإحداثِ هذا اللفظِ عندَ عروضِ الوجعِ في الصدرِ.

The second is *natural verbal indication* (*lafẓiyyah ṭabīʿiyyah*) – such as the expression "*Uḥ! Uḥ!*" (with a *hamzah* and a silent, dotless *ḥā*') signifying chest pain, as nature compels the production of this expression when experiencing such pain.

---

16   (Tr:) The three aspects are verbal, intellectual, and natural, as are then mentioned in the text.

وثالثُهـا: «اللفظيّـةُ العقليّـة» كدلالةِ لفظِ «ديزٍ» المسـموعِ مِن وراءِ الجدارِ ﴿م ٧﴾ على وجودِ اللافظِ. ﴿د ٥٩﴾

The third is *intellectual verbal indication* (*lafẓiyyah ʿaqliyyah*) – such as hearing the expression "*dīz*" from behind a wall signifying the existence of a speaker.

ورابعُهـا: «غيـرُ اللفظيّـةِ الوضعيّـةِ» كدلالةِ الـدَّوالِّ الأربـعِ على مدلولاتِها.

The fourth is *conventional non-verbal indication* (*ghayr lafẓi-yyah waḍʿiyyah*) – such as the four indicators[17] signifying what they indicate.

وخامسُهـا: «غيـرُ اللفظيّـةِ الطبيعيّـةِ» كدلالةِ صهيـلِ الفرسِ على طلبِ الماءِ والكلإِ.

The fifth is *natural non-verbal indication* (*ghayr lafẓiyyah ṭabīʿiyyah*) – such as a horse's neighing signifying its request for water and food.

وسادسُها: «غيرُ اللفظيّةِ العقليّةِ» كدلالةِ الدخانِ على النارِ. ﴿ب ١٦﴾

The sixth is *intellectual non-verbal indication* (*ghayr lafẓiyyah ʿaqliyyah*) – such as smoke signifying fire.

WHAT LOGICIANS STUDY[مباحث المنطقيّ]

فهـذهِ سـتُّ دلالاتٍ، والمنطقيُّ إنَّما يبحـثُ عن الدلالةِ اللفظيّةِ الوضعيّـةِ؛ لأنَّ الإفـادةَ للغيـرِ والاسـتفادةَ إنَّمـا يتيسَّـرُ بها بسـهولةٍ،

---

17   The four indicators include written symbols, counting on fingers, road signs, and indicators that point to a thing (Cf. al-Madīnah edition, 7 fn 1).

بـخلافِ غيرِهـا؛ فإنَّ الإفـادةَ والاستفادةَ بها لا يخلو عـن صعوبةٍ، هذا(١٨). ‹م٨، د٦٠›

These are six indications. The logician studies *conventional verbal indication* (*dalālah lafẓiyyah waḍ'iyyah*) because it facilitates communication and comprehension, unlike the other types, since they are not without difficulty in these respects. Take this.

فصلٌ [أقسامُ الدلالةِ اللفظيّةِ الوضعيّةِ]

CONVENTIONAL VERBAL
INDICATION

وينبغـي أنْ يعلـمَ أنَّ الدلالـةَ اللفظيّـةَ الوضعيّةَ التي لهـا العبرةُ في المحاوراتِ والعلومِ على ثلاثةِ أنحاءٍ.

It should be known that conventional verbal indication (*dalālah lafẓiyyah waḍ'iyyah*), which is significant in debates and sciences, has three varieties.

أحدُهـا: المطابقيّـةُ، وهـي: أنْ يـدلَّ اللفظُ على تمامِ مـا وُضِعَ ‹ب١٧› ذلـكَ اللفـظُ لـه، كدلالـةِ ‹د٦١› «الإنسانِ» على مجموعِ الحيوانِ الناطقِ.

The first is *indication by accordance* (*muṭābaqiyyah*), which is when the expression indicates exactly what the expression was designated for. An example is *human* signifying the totality of rational animal.

ثانيها: التضمّنيّةُ، وهي: أنْ يدلَّ اللفظُ على جزءِ المعنى الموضوعِ له، كدلالتِه على الحيوانِ فقطْ، أو الناطقِ فقطْ.

---

18   According to *Al-Mirḍāt*, the word (هذا) is most likely the object of an implied verb, i.e. "Take this." Cf. Dār al-Mālik, 61 fn 1.

The second is *indication by inclusion (taḍammuniyyah)*, which is when the word indicates a part of the meaning designated for it. An example is it signifying only *animal* or only *rational being*.

ثالثُها: الدلالةُ الالتزاميّةُ، وهي: أنْ لا يدلَّ اللفظُ على الموضوعِ له ولا على جزئِه، بل على معنىً خارجٍ ﴿د٦٢﴾ لازمٍ للموضوعِ له.

The third is *indication by necessary entailment (iltizāmiyyah)*, which is when an expression does not signify the meaning it was designated for [as a whole], nor a part of it, but rather an external meaning that is a *concomitant consequent (lāzim)* of what it was designated for.

واللازمُ هو: ما ينتقلُ الذهنُ مِن الموضوعِ له إليه، ﴿ب١٨﴾ كدلالةِ الإنسانِ على قابلِ العلمِ وصنعةِ الكتابةِ، وكدلالةِ لفظِ العمىٰ على البصرِ.

The *concomitant consequent (lāzim)* is what the mind transitions to from what it was designated for. For example, *human* signifying the capacity for knowledge and the craft of writing, or the expression *blindness* signifying sight.

INDICATION BY INCLUSION
AND INDICATION BY
NECESSARY ENTAILMENT

فصلٌ [في الدلالةِ التضمّنيّةِ والالتزاميّةِ]

الدلالةُ التضمّنيّةُ والالتزاميّةُ لا توجدانِ بـدونِ المطابقةِ؛ ﴿د٦٣﴾ وذلـكَ لأنَّ الجـزءَ لا يتصوّرُ بدونِ الكلِّ، وكـذا اللازمُ بدونِ الملزومِ، والتابعُ لا يوجدُ بدونِ المتبوعِ. والمطابقةُ قد توجدُ بدونِهما؛ لجوازِ أنْ يوضعَ اللفظُ لمعنىً بسيطٍ لا جزءَ له، ولا لازمَ له.

Indication by inclusion (*taḍammuniyyah*) and indication by necessary entailment (*iltizāmiyyah*) do not exist without indication by accordance (*muṭābaqiyyah*). This is because a part cannot be conceptualised without the whole, a concomitant consequent (*lāzim*) cannot exist without a concomitant antecedent (*malzūm*),[19] and the dependent (*tābiʿ*) cannot exist without that upon which it depends (*matbūʿ*). However, indication by accordance can exist without them, since it is possible for an expression to signify a simple meaning that has neither parts nor implications.

فإنْ قلتَ: لا نسلّمُ أنْ يوجدَ معنىً لا لازمَ لـه؛ فإنَّ لكلِّ معنىً لازمًا البتةَ، وأقلُّه ‹د٦٤›، أنَّه ليسَ غيرَه.

قلنـا: المـرادُ باللازمِ ‹م٩›، هـو: اللازمُ البيّنُ الذي ينتقلُ الذهنُ مِن الملزومِ إليه، ‹ب١٩›، وقولُكَ: «ليسَ غيرَه» ليسَ مِن اللوازمِ البيّنةِ؛ لأنَّا كثيرًا مـا نتصوّرُ المعانـي ولا يخطرُ ببالِنا معنى الغيـرِ فضلًا عن كونه ليسَ غيرَه.

If you were to say, "We do not accept the existence of a meaning without a concomitant consequent (*lāzim*), since every meaning has a concomitant consequent, at the least, that it is not something else."

We would respond that by *concomitant consequent* (*lāzim*) we mean the evident concomitant consequent to which the mind transitions from the concomitant antecedent. Your statement – "It is not something else" – is not an evident concomitant consequent since we often conceptualise meanings without the notion of something else coming to mind, let alone the idea that it is not something else.

---

19   (Tr:) When A implies B, B is the concomitant consequent (*lāzim*) and A is the concomitant antecedent (*malzūm*). In such a relationship, A cannot exist unaccompanied by B, though B can exist unaccompanied by A. In the example of *human* implying *knowledge*: *human* cannot exist unaccompanied by *knowledge*, though *knowledge* can exist unaccompanied by *human*.

EXPRESSIONS ARE SIMPLE OR
COMPOUND

فصلٌ [اللفظُ إمّا مفردٌ أو مركّبٌ]

اللفظُ الدالُّ إمّا مفردٌ أو مركّبٌ.

A signifying expression is either simple or compound.

فـ «المفـردُ»: ما لا يُقصدُ بجزئِه الدلالةُ على جزءٍ معناهُ، كدلالةِ همـزةِ الاسـتفهامِ علـى ‹د٥٦› معناهـا، ودلالـةِ «زيدٌ» على مسـمّاهُ، ودلالةِ «عبدِ اللَّهِ» على المعنى العلَميِّ.

A *simple signifying expression* (mufrad) is one in which its parts are not intended to signify parts of its meaning, such as the question particle (hamzat al-istifhām) signifying its meaning, *Zaid* signifying what it names, or *'Abd Allāh* signifying a proper name.

و «المركّـبُ»: مـا يُقصدُ بجزئِه الدلالـةُ على جزءٍ معناهُ، ‹ب٢٠› كدلالةِ «زيدٌ قائمٌ» على معناهُ، ودلالةِ «رامي السهمِ» على فحواه.

A *compound signifying expression* (murakkab) is one in which its parts are intended to signify parts of its meaning, such as *Zaid standing* signifying its meaning or *the one launching the arrow* signifying its intended meaning.

SIMPLE EXPRESSIONS

[أقسام المفرد]

ثمَّ المفردُ على أنحاءٍ ثلاثةٍ؛ لأنَّه إنْ كانَ معناهُ مستقلًّا بالمفهوميّةِ، أي: لـم يكـنْ في فهمِه محتاجًا إلى ضمِّ ضميمةٍ، فهو اسـمٌ إنْ لم ‹م١٠› يقتـرنْ ذلـكَ المعنى بزمانٍ مِن الأزمنةِ الثلاثةِ، ‹د٦٦› وكلمةٌ إنْ اقتـرنَ بـه، وإنْ لم يكنْ معناهُ مستقلًّا فهو أداةٌ في عـرفِ الميزانيّيـن، وحرفٌ في اصطلاحِ النحويّينِ، هذا.

The simple expression is divided into three varieties. If its meaning is independent through its conceptuality – meaning it does not require additional context for its understanding – it is a *noun* (*ism*) if that meaning is unrelated to one of the three tenses; or it is a *word* (*kalimah*) if it is related to a specific tense. However, if its meaning is not independent, it is an *operand* (*ādah*) in the terminology of logicians or a *particle* (*ḥarf*) in the terminology of grammarians.

<table>
<tr><td>"WORD" ACCORDING TO LOGICIANS</td><td>فصلٌ [الكلمةُ عندَ المناطقةِ]</td></tr>
</table>

اعلمْ أنّه قد ظنَّ بعضُهم أنَّ الكلمةَ عندَ أهلِ الميزانِ هي ما يُسمّىٰ في علمِ النحوِ بـ «الفعلِ»، وليسَ هذا الظنُّ بصوابٍ؛ فإنَّ الفعلَ أعمُّ مِن الكلمـةِ، ألا ترىٰ أنَّ نحوَ: (ب ٢١) «أضربُ» (د٦٧) و «نضربُ» وأمثالَه فعلٌ عندَ النحاةِ وليسَ بكلمةٍ عندَ المنطقيّينَ؛ لأنَّ الكلمةَ مِن أقسامِ المفردِ، ونحوِ «أضرب» ليسَ بمفردٍ، بل هو مركّبٌ لدلالةِ جزءِ اللفـظِ علىٰ جزءِ المعنىٰ؛ لأنَّ الهمزةَ تـدلُّ على المتكلّمِ، و «ض ر ب» علىٰ معنى الحدثِ. (م ١١)

Know that some have assumed that in the science of logic, *word* (*kalimah*) is equivalent to what is called *verb* (*fi'l*) in the science of grammar. This assumption is inaccurate because *verb* is broader in scope than *word*. Do you not see that *I strike* (*aḍrib*) and *We strike* (*naḍrib*) and the like are considered verbs to grammarians but not [even] words to logicians?

This is because *word* falls under the category of the simple signifying expression (*mufrad*) while the likes of *I strike* is not a simple expression. Rather, they are compound (*murakkab*), since a part of the word indicates a part of the meaning – (*'a*) indicates the speaker, while *strike* (*ḍ-r-b*) indicates the event.

 فصلٌ [تقسيمٌ آخرُ للمفردِ]

قد يقسَّمُ المفردُ بتقسيمٍ آخرَ، وهو أنَّ المفردَ قد يكونُ معناهُ واحدًا أو يكونُ كثيرًا. ﴿د٦٨﴾

The simple expression can also be classified in another way, namely, that its meanings can be singular or multiple.

والـذي لـه معنـىً واحدًا علىٰ ثلاثةِ أضربٍ؛ لأنَّه لا يخلـو إمّا أنْ يكونَ ﴿ب٢٢﴾ ذلكَ المعنىٰ متعيّنًا مشخّصًا أو لم يكنْ.

What has a single meaning falls into three subcategories, since that meaning is either identified and individuated, or not.

والأوّلُ: يُسـمَّىٰ: «علَمًا»، كـ «زيدٍ»، و «هذا»، «وهو». والأُولىٰ أنْ يُسمَّىٰ هذا القسمُ بـ «الجزئيِّ الحقيقيِّ».

The first is called *proper name* (ʿalam), such as *Zaid*, *this*, and *he*. However, it is best to refer to this category as the *genuine particular* (juzʾī ḥaqīqī).

والثاني: أي: ما لا يكونُ معناهُ مشخّصًا، بل يكونُ له أفرادٌ كثيرةٌ هو ضربانِ: ﴿د٦٩﴾

The second, meaning that its meaning is not individuated but rather has many members, is divided into two subcategories.

أحدُهما: أنْ يكونَ صدقُ ذلكَ المعنىٰ علىٰ ﴿ب٢٣﴾ سائرِ أفرادِه علىٰ سـبيلِ الاسـتواءِ، مِن غيرِ أنْ يتفاوتَ بأوّليّةٍ، أو أشدّيّةٍ، أو أزيدّيّةٍ، ويُسمّىٰ هذا القسمُ بـ «المتواطئ»؛ لتواطؤ أفرادِه، وتوافقِها في تصادقِ ذلكَ المعنى العامِّ، كالإنسانِ بالنسبةِ إلىٰ زيدٍ وعمرٍو وبكرٍ.

The first is when the general meaning applies equally to all members without any variation in terms of priority, intensity, or precedence. This type is called *equipollent* (*muṭawāṭiʾ*) because its members align and agree in their mutual application (*taṣāduq*) with the general meaning. For example, *human* in relation to Zaid, ʿAmr, and Bakr.

وثانيهمــا: أنْ لا يكــونَ صــدقُ ذلكَ المعنى العامُّ في بقيعِ أفرادِه على وجهِ الاســتواءِ، بل يكونُ صدقُ ذلكَ المعنى على بعضِ الأفرادِ بالأوّليّـةِ، والأشـدّيّـةِ، والأولويّـةِ، وصدقُها على البعضِ الآخرِ بأضدادِ ذلكَ، كالوجودِ بالنسبةِ إلى الواجبِ جلَّ (م١٢) مجدُه، وبالنسبةِ إلى الممكنِ، وكالبياضِ بالنسبةِ إلى الثلجِ والعاجِ، ويُسـمّى هذا القسمُ: «مشـكّكًا»؛ لأنَّه يوقعُ الناظرَ في الشـكِّ (ب٢٤) في كونِه متواطئًا أو مشتركًا. (د٠٧)

The second is when the general meaning does not apply equally for all its members. Rather, its truth holds for some members with priority, intensity, or precedence, while for others, it applies to a lesser degree. For example, *existence* in relation to the Necessary (Glorious be His Majesty) as opposed to possible beings, and *whiteness* in relation to snow and ivory. This is called *gradational* [or: *non-equipollent*] (*mushakkik*) because it causes uncertainty in the observer as to whether it is equipollent (*muṭawāṭiʾ*) or homonymous (*mushtarak*).

<table>
<tr><td></td><td>فصلٌ [في أقسامِ اللفظ المتكثّرِ المعنى]</td></tr>
</table>

المتكثّرُ المعنى له أقسامٌ عديدةٌ.

Expressions with multiple meanings have numerous categories.

وجهُ الحصرِ: أنَّ اللفظَ الذي كَثُرَ معناهُ إنْ وُضِعَ ذلكَ اللفظُ لكلِّ معنىً ابتداءً بأوضاعٍ متعدّدةٍ على حِدّةٍ يُسمّى: «مشـتركًا»، كالعينِ وُضِـعَ تـارةً للذهبِ، وتـارةً للباصرةِ، وتارةً للركبـةِ. وإنْ لم يوضعْ لكلٍّ ابتـداءً، بـل وُضِـعَ أوّلًا لمعنـىً، ثمَّ استُعملَ في معنىً ثاني؛ لأجلِ مناسبةٍ بينَهما: فإنْ اشـتُهرَ في الثاني، وتركَ موضوعَه الأوّلَ يُسـمّى: «منقولًا».

The basis for this classification is as follows: when an expression has numerous meanings, if it was initially designated for each meaning separately, it is called *homonymous* (*mushtarak*). An example is *'ayn*, which is at times designated for gold, at times for the organ of sight, and at times for the kneecap.

However, if it was not initially designated for each meaning separately, but rather was first designated for one meaning and later used for another due to a relation between them, and if it then became well-known for the second meaning while its original designation for the first was abandoned, it is called *transferred* (*manqūl*).

والمنقولُ بالنظرِ إلى الناقلِ ينقسمُ إلى ثلاثةِ أقسامٍ:

Transferred expressions, with respect to the agent of transference, are divided into three categories.

أحدُها: «المنقولُ العرفيُّ»، باعتبارِ كونِ الناقلِ عرفًا عامًّا.

The first is *conventional transfer* (*manqūl 'urfī*), based on the transferrer being general convention.

وثانيها: «المنقولُ الشرعيُّ»، باعتبارِ كونِه أربابَ (م١٣) الشرعِ.

The second is *legislative transfer* (*manqūl shar'ī*), based on the transferrer being religious authority.

وثالثُهـا: «المنقـولُ الاصطلاحـيُّ»، (د٧٢) باعتبـارِه عرفًا خاصًّا بطائفةٍ مخصوصةٍ. (ب٢٥)

The third is *terminological transfer (manqūl iṣṭilāḥī)*, based on it being a specific convention within a specific group.

مثـالُ الأوّلِ: كلفظِ «الدابّةِ»، كانَ في الأصلِ موضوعًا لِما يدبُّ على الأرضِ، نقلَه العامّةُ للفرسِ أو لذاتِ القوائمِ الأربع.

An example of the first [i.e. conventional transfer] is the expression *dābbah*, which was initially designated for what creeps on the ground, but the common public transferred it to horses or any four-legged animal.

ومثـالُ الثاني: كلفظِ «الـصلاةِ»، كانَ في الأصلِ بمعنى الدعاءِ، ثمَّ نقلَه الشارعُ إلىٰ أركانٍ مخصوصةٍ.

An example of the second [i.e. legislative transfer] is the expression *ṣalāt*, which initially meant "supplication," but the Legislator transferred it to signify [an act possessing] specified pillars.

ومثـالُ الثالـثِ: كلفظِ «الاسمِ» كانَ في اللغةِ بمعنـى العلوِّ، ثمَّ نقلَه النحاةُ إلىٰ كلمةٍ مستقلّةٍ في الدلالةِ غيرِ مقترنةٍ بزمانٍ مِن الأزمنةِ الثلاثةِ.

An example of the third [i.e. terminological transfer] is the expression *ism* which, in the language, initially meant "elevation." Then grammarians transferred it to [mean] a word that indicates on its own and is unaccompanied by one of the three tenses.

وإنْ لم يُشتهرْ في الثاني ولم يُتركْ الأوّلُ، بل يستعملُ في الموضوعِ الأوّلِ مرّةً، وفي الثاني أخرىٰ، يُسـمّىٰ بالنسبةِ إلى الأوّلِ: «حقيقةً»، وبالنسـبةِ إلـى الثاني «مجازًا»، (م ١٤) كالأسدِ بالنسبةِ إلى الحيوانِ المفترسِ والرجلِ الشـجاعِ، فهو بالنسبةِ إلى الأوّلِ حقيقةٌ، وبالنسـبةِ إلى الثاني مجازٌ.

If it does not become well-known for the second meaning and the first is not abandoned – rather, it is used for the first designated meaning at times and for the second at others – then it is called *literal* (*ḥaqīqah*) with respect to the first and *figurative* (*majāz*) with respect to the second.

For example, *lion* with respect to the predatory animal and a brave man – where it is literal for the first and figurative for the second.

SYNONYMOUS EXPRESSIONS   فصلٌ [في اللفظِ المرادفِ]

إذا كانَ اللفظُ متعدِّدًا والمعنى واحدًا يُسـمّى: «مرادفًا»، كالأسـدِ والليثِ، والغيمِ^(٢٠) (د ٧٢) والغيثِ. (ب ٢٦)

When multiple expressions have the same meaning, it is called *synonymous* (*murādif*). An example is *asad* and *layth* for *lion*, and *maṭar* and *ghayth* for *rain*.

COMPOUND EXPRESSIONS   فصلٌ [في أقسامِ المركّبِ]

المركّبُ قسمانِ.

Compound expressions are divided into two parts.

أحدُهمـا: «المركّبُ التـامُّ»، وهـو: ما يصحُّ السـكوتُ عليه، كـ «زيدٌ قائمٌ».

The first is the *complete compound* (*murakkab tāmm*), which is what it is valid to pause after.[21] For example: *Zaid is standing.*

---

20   This most likely is a slip of the pen since *ghaym* means clouds whereas *al-ghayth* means rain. This is why I have translated it as *al-maṭr*. Cf. al-Madīnah edition, 15 fn 2.

21   (Tr:) i.e. one can come to a full stop as it conveys a complete meaning.

وثانيهِما: «المركّبُ الناقصُ»، وهو: ما ليسَ كذلكَ.

The second is the *incomplete compound* (*murakkab nāqiṣ*), what is otherwise.

فصلٌ [في أقسامِ التامِّ]

THE COMPLETE COMPOUND

المركّبُ التامُّ ضربانِ.

The complete compound is divided into two parts.

يُقالُ لأحدِهما: «الخبرُ» و «القضيّةُ»، وهو: ما قُصدَ به الحكايةُ، ‹د٧٣› ويحتمِلُ الصدقَ والكذبَ، أو ما يُقالُ لقائلِه: إنّه صادقٌ أو كاذبٌ، نحوُ: السماءُ فوقَنا، والعالَمُ حادثٌ.

The first is called a *declarative statement* (*khabar*) or a *proposition* (*qaḍiyyah*). It is what is intended to convey information and is conceivable to be true or false, or it can be said of its speaker that he is truthful or lying. For example: *The sky is above us* and *The world is originated.*

فإنْ قيلَ: قولُنا: «لا إلـهَ إلّا اللَّهُ» قضيّةٌ وخبرٌ، مع أنّه لا يحتملُ الكذبَ. قلتُ: مجرّدُ ‹م١٥› اللفـظِ يحتملُه، وإنْ كانَ بالنظرِ إلىٰ خصوصيّةِ الحاشيتَينِ غيرُ محتملٍ للكذبِ.

Suppose it is said that our statement *There is no deity except Allah* is a proposition (*qaḍiyyah*) and a declarative statement (*khabar*), despite it not being conceivable as false. I respond that the bare expression is conceivable as such, even if, in terms of the specificity of its contents, it is not conceivable for it to be false.

ويُقالُ لثاني القسـمينِ: «الإنشاءُ»، والإنشاءُ أقسامٌ: أمرٌ، ونهيٌ، وتمنٍّ، وترجٍّ، ‹د٧٤› واستفهامٌ، ونداءٌ.

The second category can be referred to as *performative* (*inshā'*). Performative statements include several subcategories: command, prohibition, wish, request, interrogative, and invocation.[22]

THE INCOMPLETE COMPOUND

فصلٌ [في أقسامِ الناقصِ]

المركّبُ الناقصُ على أنحاءٍ.

مِنْها: «المركّبُ الإضافيُّ»، كـ «غلامِ زيدٍ». (ب٢٧)

ومِنْها: «المركّبُ التوصيفيُّ»، كـ «الرجلِ العالِمِ».

ومِنْها «المركّبُ التقييديُّ»، كـ «في الدارِ».

The incomplete compound (*murakkab nāqiṣ*) is divided into varieties, including:

- The *attributive compound* (*murakkab iḍāfī*), such as: *Zaid's boy.*
- The *descriptive compound* (*murakkab tawṣīfī*), such as: *The knowledgeable man.*
- The *restrictive compound* (*murakkab taqyīdī*), such as: *in the house.*

* * *

وهاهنا قد تمَّ بحثُ الألفاظِ، والآنَ أرشدُكَ إلى بحثِ المعاني.

With this, we have discussed the forms of expressions. Now I will guide you to the study of meanings.

---

22 (Tr:) Performative statements (*inshā'*) are non-propositional utterances to which truth and falsehood do not apply.

فصلٌ [في أقسامِ المفهومِ]

المفهــومُ، أي: مــا حصلَ في الذهنِ، قســمانِ. أحدُهما: جزئيٌّ. والثاني: كلّيٌّ.

A *concept* (*mafhūm*) – meaning what is apprehended in the mind – is of two categories: one is *particular* (*juz'ī*) and the other is *universal* (*kullī*).

أمّا «الجزئيُّ» فهو: ما يمنعُ نفسُ تصوّرِه عن صدقِه علىٰ كثيرٍ، كـ «زيدٍ» و «عمرٍو»، و«هذا الفرسِ» «م١٦، د٥٥٧»، و «هذا الجدارِ».

A *particular* (*juz'ī*) is that whose very conception prevents it from being truly predicated of multiple instances. For example: *Zaid, 'Amr, this horse*, and *this wall*.

وأمّا «الكلّيُّ» فهو: ما لا يمنعُ نفسُ تصوّرِه عن وقوعِ الشركةِ فيه، وعن صدقِه علىٰ كثيرينَ، كالإنسانِ والفرسِ. (ب٢٨)

A *universal* (*kullī*) is that whose very conception does not prevent multiplicity in its instantiation or its true predication of multiple instances. For example: *human* and *horse*.

وقد يُفسَّرُ الكلّيُّ والجزئيُّ بتفسيرينِ آخرينِ. أمّا الكلّيُّ: فهو ما جوّزَ العقلُ تكثّرَه مِن حيثُ تصوّرُه. وأمّا الجزئيُّ: فهو ما لا يكونُ كذلكَ. (م١٧)

Universal and particular can be explained in two other ways: a *universal* (*kullī*) is what the intellect deems capable of multiplicity insofar as it is conceptualised; and a *particular* (*juz'ī*) is that which is not so.

فصلٌ [أقسامُ الكلّيِّ]

الكلّيُّ أقسامٌ.

The universal is divided into several categories.

أحدُها: ما يمتنـعُ وجودُ أفرادِه في الخارِجِ، ‹د٧٦› كاللاشـيءٍ، واللامُمكِنِ، واللاموجودِ.

The first is that whose instances cannot exist in external actuality (*fi al-khārij*),[23] such as a non-being, an impossible being, and a nonexistent being.

وثانيهمـا: مـا يمكـنُ أفـرادُه ولـم توجـدْ، كالعنقـاءٍ، وجبـلٍ مِن الياقوت. ‹ب٢٩›

The second is that whose instances are possible but have not come into existence, such as a phoenix and a mountain made of sapphire.

وثالثُهمـا: مـا أمكنـتْ أفرادُه ولم يوجـدْ مِن أفـرادِه إلّا فردٌ واحدٌ، كالشمسِ، والواجبِ تعالىٰ.

The third is that whose instances could exist, yet only a single instance exists, such as the Sun and the Necessary Being (Most High is He).

ورابعُها: ما وُجدتْ له أفرادٌ كثيرةٌ. إمّا متناهيّةً، كالكواكبِ السيّارةِ ‹م١٨› فإنّهـا سبعٌ: الشـمسُ، والقمرُ، والمريـخُ، والزهـرةُ، والزحلُ، وعطاردُ، والمشـتريُ. أو غيرَ متناهيةٍ كأفرادِ ‹د٧٧› الإنسـانِ، والفرسِ، والغنمِ، والبقرِ.

---

23   (Tr:) This "existence outside the mind" can also be referred to as being "extra-mental," "objective," or "in reality."

The fourth is what has multiple existent instances, which are either finite – such as the wandering celestial bodies (*kawākib sayyārah*), which are seven: the sun, the Moon, Mars, Venus, Saturn, Mercury, and Jupiter – infinite, such as the instances of humans, horses, sheep, and cattle.

وقــد أُورِدَ علـىٰ تعريفِ الكلّيِّ والجزئيِّ سـؤالٌ، تقريـرُه: أنَّ الصورةَ الحاصلـةَ مِـن البيضةِ المعيّنةِ، والشـبح المرئي مِن بعيدٍ، ومحسـوسِ الطفـلِ فـي مبـدأِ الولادةِ كلَّها جزئيّاتٌ، مع أنَّـه يصدقُ عليها تعريفُ الكلّيِّ؛ لأنَّ في هذهِ الصورِ فرضَ صدقِها علىٰ كثيرينَ غيرُ ممتنعٍ.

والجوابُ: أنَّ المرادَ بصدقِ المفهومِ في تعريفِ الكلّيِّ هو الصدقُ علـىٰ وجهِ الاجتمـاعِ، وهذهِ الصـورُ – أعني: صـورةَ البيضـةِ المعيّنةِ وغيرَها – إنَّمـا يصـدقُ علىٰ كثيرينَ بدلًا لا معًا، فإنَّ الوحدةَ مأخوذةٌ فـي هـذهِ الصورِ ضرورةَ أنَّها مأخوذةٌ مِـن مادّةٍ معيّنةٍ جزئيّةٍ، ولولا فيها اعتبارُ التوحّدِ لكانتْ كلّيّةً مِن غيرِ لزومِ أشكالٍ، هذا. (١٩م، ب٣٠)

A question is raised concerning the definition of the universal (*kullī*) and the particular (*juz'ī*), formulated as follows:

An image formed from a specific egg, a distant apparition, and a child's initial sensations at birth are all particulars, yet the definition of the universal applies to them. This is because it is not impossible to assume their true predication of multiple instances.[24]

The answer is that what is meant by true predication (*ṣidq*) in the definition of the universal (*kullī*) is predication in a simultaneous sense (*'alā wajh al-ijtimā'*). These images – i.e. the image of a specific egg and others – are predicated of multiple instances successively, not simultaneously. That is, unity is necessarily included in these images because they are derived from a specified particular (*juz'ī*) matter (*māddah*). Were it not for this

---

24   See al-Madīnah edition, 19; al-Bushrā edition, 30.

consideration of unity, they would be universal without entailing any complications (*min ghayr luzūm ashkāl*).

This is the explanation.

THE RELATIONSHIP BETWEEN TWO
UNIVERSALS

فصلٌ: في النسبةِ بين الكلّيّين

اعلـمْ أنَّ النسـبةَ بيــنَ الكلّيّينِ تتصوّرُ علىٰ أنحاءٍ أربعةٍ: لأنَّكَ إذا أخذتَ كلّيّينِ، ﴿د٧٨﴾ فإمّا

Know that the relationship between two universals can be conceptualised in four ways. This is because when you take two universals, either:

(١) أنْ يصـدقَ كلٌّ مِنهمـا علىٰ كلِّ ما يصدقُ عليه الآخرُ فهُما متساويانِ، كالإنسانِ والناطقِ، لأنَّ كلَّ إنسانٍ ناطقٌ، وكلَّ ناطقٍ إنسانٌ.

(1) Each one is truly predicated of everything the other is predicated of – in which case, they are *equivalent* (*mutasāwiyān*), such as *human* and *rational being*, since every human is a rational being and every rational being is a human.

(٢) أو يصـدقَ أحدُهمـا علـىٰ كلِّ مـا يصـدقُ عليـه الآخرُ، ولا يصـدقُ الآخـرُ علىٰ جميعِ أفـرادِ أحدِهما، فبينَهمـا عمومٌ وخصوصٌ مطلـقٌ، كالحيوانِ والإنسانِ، فيصـدقُ الحيوانُ علىٰ كلِّ ما يصدقُ عليه الإنسانُ، ولا يصدقُ الإنسانُ علىٰ كلِّ ما يصدقُ عليه الحيوانِ، بل علىٰ بعضِه.

(2) One is truly predicated of everything the other is predicated of, while one is not truly predicated of all instances of the first – in which case, the relationship between them is *absolute universality and particularity* (*'umūm wa khuṣūṣ muṭlaq*, superset

and set), such as *animal* and *human*: *animal* is truly predicated of everything *human* is predicated of, and *human* is truly predicated of only some of what *animal* is predicated of.

(٣) أو لا يصدقَ شيءٌ مِنْهما على شيءٍ بما يصدقُ عليه الآخرُ، فهُما متباينانِ، كالإنسانِ والفرسِ. (ب٣١)

(3) Neither one is truly predicated of anything the other is predicated of – in which case, they are *mutually exclusive (mutabāyanān)*, such as *human* and *horse*.

(٤) أو يصدقَ بعضُ كلِّ واحدٍ مِنْهما على بعضٍ ما يصدقُ عليه الآخرُ، فبينَهما عمومٌ وخصوصٌ مِن وجهٍ، (د٧٩) كالأبيضِ والحيوانِ ففي البطِّ يصدقُ كلٌّ مِنْهما، وفي الفيلِ يصدقُ الحيوانُ فقطْ، وفي الثلجِ والعاجِ يصدقُ الأبيضُ فقطْ.

(4) Part of each is truly predicated of part of what the other is predicated of – in which case, the relationship between them is *partial overlap (‘umūm wa khuṣūṣ min wajh)*, such as *white* and *animal*: both *white* and *animal* are truly predicated of a duck, only *animal* is truly predicated of an elephant, and only *white* is truly predicated of snow and ivory.

فهذهِ أربعُ نسبٍ: التساوي، والتباينِ، والعمومِ والخصوصِ المطلقِ، والعمومِ والخصوصِ مِن وجهٍ. فاحفظْ ذلكَ. (م٢٠)

These are the four relationships:
1. Equivalence (*mutasāwiyān*)
2. Mutual exclusivity (*mutabāyanān*)
3. Absolute universality and particularity (*‘umūm wa khuṣūṣ muṭlaq*)
4. Partial overlap (*‘umūm wa khuṣūṣ min wajh*)
   Commit this to memory.

ANOTHER MEANING OF THE PARTICULAR فصلٌ [معنىٰ آخرُ للجزئيِّ]

قد يُقالُ للجزئيِّ معنىٰ آخرُ، وهو: ما كانَ أخصُّ تحتَ الأعمِّ.

Another meaning of *particular* (*juz'ī*) [the *attributive particular* is] is what is more specific within a more general category.

فـ «الإنسانُ» علىٰ هذا التعريفِ جزئيٌّ؛ لدخولِه تحتَ الحيوانِ، وكـذا الحيوانُ؛ لدخولِه تحتَ الجسـمِ النامي، وكذا الجسـمُ النامي؛ لدخولِه تحتَ الجسمِ المطلقِ، وكذا الجسمُ المطلقِ؛ لدخولِه تحتَ الجوهرِ.

So, according to this definition, *human* is a particular because it falls under *animal*.

And *animal* is a particular because it falls under *animate body*.

And *animate body* is a particular because it falls under *absolute body*.

And *absolute body* is a particular because it falls under *substance*.

والنسبةُ بينَ الجزئيِّ الحقيقيِّ وبينَ هذا المسمّىٰ بـ «الجزئيِّ الإضافيِّ» عمومٌ وخصوصٌ مطلقًا؛ لاجتماعِهما في «زيدٍ» مثلًا، وصدقِ الإضافيِّ بـدونِ الحقيقيِّ فـي «الإنسـانِ»؛ فإنَّه جزئيٌّ إضافيٌّ، وليـسَ بجزئيٍّ حقيقيٍّ؛ لأنَّ صدقَه علىٰ كثيرينَ غيرُ ممتنعٍ. (ب٣٢، د٨٠)

The relationship between the *genuine particular* (*juz'ī ḥaqīqī*) and what is called the *attributive particular* (*juz'ī iḍāfī*) is one of absolute universality and particularity [superset and set]. This is because they coexist in *Zaid*, for example, while the attributive particular – but not the genuine particular – is true for *human*. This is because *human* is an attributive particular and not a genuine particular, as its true predication of multiple instances is not impossible.

[الكليات «الجنس»]

THE FIVE UNIVERSALS

فصلٌ [الأول من الكليات «الجنس»]

THE FIRST UNIVERSAL: GENUS

الكلّيّاتُ خمسٌ.

There are five universals (*kulliyyāt*).

الأوّلُ: «الجنسُ»، كلّيٌّ مقولٌ على كثيرينَ مختلفينَ في الحقائقِ في جوابِ «ما هو»، كـ«الحيوانِ» فإنَّه مقولٌ على الإنسانِ، والفرسِ، والغنمِ، إذا سُئِلَ عنها بـ «ما هي»؟، ويُقالُ: «الإنسانُ والفرسُ ما هما»؟ فالجوابُ: حيوانٌ. (م ٢١)

The first is *genus* (*jins*) – a universal concept predicated of many things that differ in their realities, in response to the question "What is it?" (*mā huwa?*) For example: *animal*, which is predicated of humans, horses, and sheep when one asks them, "What is it?"

Likewise, if one were to ask, "What are humans and horses?" the answer would be *animals*.

فصلٌ [الثاني من الكليات «النوع»]

THE SECOND UNIVERSAL: SPECIES

الثاني: «النوعُ»، وهو: كلّيٌّ مقولٌ (د ٨١) على كثيرينَ متّفقينَ بالحقائقِ في جوابِ «ما هو».

The second is the *species* (*nawʿ*) – a universal concept predicated of many things that share the same reality (*ḥaqīqah*), in response to the question "What is it?" (*mā huwa?*)

وللنوعِ معنى آخرُ، ويُقالُ له: «النوعُ الإضافيُّ»، وهو: ماهيّةٌ يُقالُ عليها وعلى غيرِها: «الجنسُ» في جوابِ «ما هو». (ب ٣٣)

Species also has another meaning, which is called the *attributive species* (*nawʿ iḍāfī*). It is a quiddity (*māhiyyah*) of which *genus* (*jins*) is predicated – both of it and others – in response to "What is it?"

وبيـنَ النـوعِ الحقيقيِّ والنوعِ الإضافيِّ عمـومٌ وخصوصٌ مِن وجهٍ؛ لتصادقِهمـا علـى الإنسـانِ، وصدقِ الحقيقيِّ بـدونِ الإضافيِّ في «النُّقطةِ»، وصدقِ ﴿د٨٢﴾ الإضافيِّ بدونِ الحقيقيِّ في الحيوانِ. ﴿م٢٢﴾

The relationship between the genuine species and the attributive species is one of partial overlap: both apply to *human*; the genuine species, but not the attributive species, is applicable to *geometric point* (*nuqṭah*); and the attributive species, but not the genuine species, is applicable to *animal*.

فصلٌ: في ترتيبِ الأجناسِ

THE CLASSIFICATION OF GENERA

الجنـسُ إمّـا «سـافلٌ»، وهو ما لا يكونُ تحتَه جنسٌ، ويكونُ فوقَه جنسٌ، بـل إنَّما يكونُ تحتَه النوعُ. كالحيوانِ فإنَّه تحتَه الإنسـانُ وهو نوعٌ، وفوقَه الجسمُ النامي وهو جنسٌ، فالحيوانُ جنسٌ سافلٌ.

A genus is either [lowest, intermediate, or highest].

A *lowest genus* (*sāfil*) is one that has no genus below it but has a genus above it, while still having a species below it. For example, *animal*, since *human* is below it as a species, while *animate body* is above it as a genus. Thus, *animal* is a lowest genus.

وإمّـا «متوسّـطٌ»، وهـو مـا يكـونُ تحتَه جنسٌ، وفوقَـه أيضًا جنسٌ. كالجسمِ النامي فإنَّ تحتَه الحيوانُ، وفوقَه الجسمُ المطلقُ. ﴿ب٣٤﴾

An *intermediate genus* (*mutawassiṭ*) is one that has both a genus above it and a genus below it. For example, *animate body*, since *animal* is below it, while *absolute body* is above it.

وإمّـا «عالـي»، وهـو مـا لا يكونُ فوقَـه جنسٌ، ويُسـمّى بـ «جنسِ الأجنـاسِ». كالجوهرِ فإنَّه ليسَ فوقَه جنسٌ، وتحتَه الجسمُ المطلقُ والجسمُ النامي والحيوانُ.

A *highest genus* (*ʿālī*) is one that has no genus above it and is called the *genus of genera* (*jins al-ajnās*). For example, *substance* has no genus above it, while below it are *absolute body*, *animate body*, and *animal*.

 فصلٌ [الأجناسُ العاليةُ عشرةٌ]

الأجناسُ العاليةُ عشرةٌ، ‹د٨٣› وليسَ في العالمِ شيءٌ خارجٌ عن هـذهِ الأجنـاسِ، ويقـالُ هـذهِ الأجناسُ العاليـةُ: «المقولاتُ العشرُ» أيضًا. أحدُها: الجوهرُ، والباقي المقولاتُ التسعُ للعَرَضِ.

The *high genera* (*ajnās ʿāliyah*) are ten, and nothing in the world is outside these genera. These high genera are also called the *Ten Categories* (*maqūlāt ʿashr*). The first of them is substance (*jawhar*), while the remaining nine categories pertain to accidents (*ʿaraḍ*).

والجوهرُ: هـو الموجـودُ لا في موضوعٍ، أي: محـلٌّ، بل هو قائمٌ بنفسِهِ، كالأجسامِ. ‹م٢٣›

A *substance* (*jawhar*) is that which exists not in a subject (*mawḍūʿ*) – meaning a substratum (*maḥall*) – but rather is self-subsistent, such as bodies.

والعَرَضُ: هو الموجودُ في موضوعٍ، أي: محلٌّ.

An *accident* (*ʿaraḍ*) is what exists in a subject (*mawḍūʿ*) – meaning a substratum (*maḥall*).

والمقـولاتُ العرضيّـةُ هـي: الكـمُّ، والكيفُ، ‹ب٣٥، د٨٤› والإضافـةُ، والأينُ، والملـكُ، والفعلُ، والانفعـالُ، والمتىٰ، والوضعُ. ‹د٨٥› ويجمعُها هذا البيتُ الفارسيُّ ‹م٢٤›

The categories which are accidents (*maqūlāt 'araḍiyyah*) are:

<table>
<tr><td>2.</td><td>Quantity (kamm)</td><td>7.</td><td>Action (fa'l)</td></tr>
<tr><td>3.</td><td>Quality (kayf)</td><td>8.</td><td>Passion (infi'āl)</td></tr>
<tr><td>4.</td><td>Relation (iḍāfah)</td><td>9.</td><td>Time (matā)</td></tr>
<tr><td>5.</td><td>Place (ayn)</td><td>10.</td><td>Position (waḍ')</td></tr>
<tr><td>6.</td><td>Possession (milk)</td><td></td><td></td></tr>
</table>

These are grouped in the Persian verse:

مردیٔ دراز نيكو ديدم به شـهر امروز * باخواسـته نشسـته از كرِد خويش فيروز

I saw a tall pious person in the city today; he was sitting with his desired possession, having successfully completed his task.

THE CLASSIFICATION OF SPECIES   فصلٌ: في ترتيبِ الأنواعِ

اعلمْ أنَّ الأنواعَ قد ترتَّبَ متنازلةً.

Know that species (*anwā'*) can be classified hierarchically.

فالنــوعُ قــد يكونُ تحتَه نوعٌ ولا يكونُ فوقَــه نوعٌ (ب٣٦)، فهو النوعُ العالي.

A species may have another species below it but no species above it. This is the *highest species* (*naw' 'ālī*).

وقد يكونُ تحتَه نوعٌ، وفوقَه نوعٌ، وهو النوعُ المتوسّطُ.

It may have a species below it and a species above it. This is the *intermediate species* (*naw' mutawassiṭ*).

وقــد لا يكــونُ تحتَــه نــوعٌ، ويكونُ فوقَه نــوعٌ، وهو النوعُ الســافلُ. (د٨٦) ويُقالُ له: نوعُ الأنواعِ أيضًا.

It may have no species below it but have a species above it. This is the *lowest species* (*naw' sāfil*), which is also called the *species of species* (*naw' al-anwā'*).

فصلٌ [الثالث من الكليات «الفصل»]

الثالثُ: «الفصلُ»، وهو: كلّيٌّ مقولٌ على الشيءِ في جوابِ «أيُّ شيءٍ هو في ذاتِه».

كما إذا سُئِلَ: «الإنسانُ أيُّ شيءٍ هو في ذاتِه»؟ فيجابُ بأنَّه ناطقٌ.

The third is the *differentia* (*faṣl*), which is a universal predicated of a thing in response to the question: "What is it in its essence?" (*ayyu shay' huwa fī dhātihi?*).

For example, if someone asks, "What is *human* in its essence?," the answer is *rational* (*nāṭiq*).

وهو قسمانِ: (ب٣٧) قريبٌ، وبعيدٌ. (م٢٥)

It is divided into two parts: proximate (*qarīb*), and remote (*ba'īd*).

فـ «القريبُ»: (د٨٧) هو المميِّزُ عن المشاركاتِ في الجنسِ القريبِ.

The *proximate differentia* (*faṣl qarīb*) is that which distinguishes something from those that share the same proximate genus.

و «البعيدُ»: هو المميِّزُ عن المشاركاتِ في الجنسِ البعيدِ.

The *remote differentia* (*faṣl ba'īd*) is that which distinguishes something from those that share the same remote genus.

فالأوَّلُ: كالناطقِ للإنسانِ. والثاني: كالحسّاسِ له.

The first is *rational* for *human*, and the second is *sensory* for *human*.

CONSTITUTIVE AND DIVISIVE
DIFFERENTIAE

[الفصلُ المقوّمُ والمقسِّمُ]

وللفصلِ نسـبةٌ إلى النوعِ فيُسـمّىٰ «مقوِّمًا»؛ لدخولِه في قِوامِ النوعِ وحقيقتِهِ، ونسبةٌ إلى الجنسِ فيُسـمّىٰ «مقسِّمًا»؛ لأنَّه يُقسِّمُ الجنسَ ويُحصِّلُ قسمًا له.

The differentia has a relation to the species, in which case it is called a *constitutive differentia* (*muqawwim*), because it falls within the *constitution* (*qiwām*) and reality (*ḥaqīqah*) of the species. And it has a relation to the genus. It is called a *divisive differentia* (*muqassim*) because it divides the genus and establishes a division within it.

كـ «الناطقِ» فهو مقوّمٌ للإنسانِ؛ لأنَّ الإنسانَ هو الحيوانُ الناطقُ، ومقسِّـمٌ للحيــوانِ؛ لأنَّ بالناطـقِ حصـلَ للحيوانِ قسـمانِ. أحدُهما: الحيوانُ الناطقُ، والثاني: الحيوانُ الغيرُ الناطقِ.

For example: *rational being* is a constitutive differentia for *human*, because *human* is *rational animal*. And it is a divisive differentia for *animal*, because through *rational*, the genus *animal* is divided into two divisions: the first, *rational animals*, and the second, *non-rational animals*.

CONSTITUTIVE DIFFERENTIAE
TRAVEL DOWNWARDS

فصلٌ [كلُّ مقوّمٍ للعالي مقوّمٌ للسافلِ]

كلُّ مقوّمٍ للعالي مقوّمٌ للسافلِ، ‹د٨٨› كالقابلِ للأبعادِ؛ فإنّه مقوّمٌ للجسمِ، وهو مقوّمٌ للجسمِ النامي، والحيوانِ، والإنسانِ. وكالنامي؛ فإنّه كما أنّه مقوّمٌ للجسمِ النامي مقوّمٌ ‹م٢٦› للحيوانِ ومقوّمٌ للإنسانِ أيضًا. وكالحسّاسِ والمتحرّكُ بالإرادةِ؛ فإنّهما كما أنّهما مقومانِ للحيوانِ كذلكَ مقومانِ للإنسانِ. ‹ب٣٨›

Every constitutive differentia (*muqawwim*) for the higher is a constitutive differentia for the lower – such as being receptive to dimensionality, which is a constitutive differentia for body and likewise for animate body, animal, and human.

And such as *animate*, which just as it is a constitutive differentia for animate body is also a constitutive differentia for animal and for human.

And such as *sensory* and *voluntary motion*, which just as they are constitutive differentiae for animal are likewise constitutive differentiae for human.

وليسَ كلُّ مقوّمٍ للسافلِ مقوّمًا للعالي؛ فإنَّ الناطقَ مقوّمٌ للإنسانِ وليسَ مقوّمًا للحيوانِ.

However, not every constitutive differentia for the lower is a constitutive differentia for the higher. For example, *rational* is a constitutive differentia for *human*, but not a constitutive differentia for *animal*.

فصلٌ [كلُّ مقسِّمٍ للسافلِ مقسِّمٌ للعالي]

كلُّ فصلٍ مقسِّمٍ للسافلِ مقسِّمٌ للعالي.

Every divisive differentia (*faṣl muqassim*) that divides the lower is also a divisive differentia for the higher.

فالناطقُ كما يقسِّمُ الحيوانَ إلى الناطقِ وغيرِ الناطقِ، كذلكَ يقسِّمُ الجسمَ إليهما.

For example, just as *rational* divides *animal* into *rational* and *non-rational*, it likewise divides *body* into these two.

وليسَ كلُّ مقسِّمٍ للعالي مقسِّمًا للسافلِ؛ فإنَّ «الحسّاسَ» مثلًا يقسِّمُ «الجسمَ النامي» إلى: «الجسمِ النامي الحسّاسِ»، و «الجسمِ النامي الغيرِ الحسّاسِ»، وليسَ يقسِّمُ «الحيوانَ» إليهما؛ فإنَّ كلَّ حيوانٍ حسّاسٌ، ولا يوجدُ حيوانٌ غيرُ حسّاسٍ.

However, not every divisive differentia for the higher is a divisive differentia for the lower. For example, *sensory* divides *animate body* into *sensitive animate body* and *non-sensitive animate body*, but it does not divide *animal* into these two. This is because every animal is sensitive, and there is no non-sensitive animal.

فصلٌ [الرابع من الكليات «الخاصة»]

الكلّيُّ الرابعُ: «الخاصّة»، وهو كلّيٌّ خارجٌ عن حقيقةِ الأفرادِ، محمولٌ على أفرادٍ واقعةٍ (د٨٩) تحتَ حقيقةٍ واحدةٍ فقطْ، كـ«الضاحكِ» للإنسانِ، و «الكاتبِ» له. (م٢٧)

THE FIFTH UNIVERSAL: GENERAL ACCIDENT

The fourth universal is the *proprium* (khāṣṣah), which is a universal that is external to the reality (ḥaqīqah) of its instances but is predicated only of instances falling under a single reality (ḥaqīqah), such as *laughing* and *writing* for *human*.

فصلٌ [الخامسُ مِن الكليّاتِ «العرض العام»]

الخامــسُ مِـن الكليّـاتِ: «العَـرَضُ العـامُّ»، وهو: الكلّـيُّ الخارجُ المقـولُ علـىٰ أفرادِ حقيقةٍ واحـدةٍ وعلىٰ غيرِها، كالماشـي المحمولِ علىٰ أفرادِ الإنسانِ والفرسِ. (ب٣٩)

The fifth universal is the *general accident* (ʿaraḍ ʿāmm), which is a universal external to the reality (ḥaqīqah) that is predicated of instances of a single reality as well as of others.

For example, *walking* is predicated of instances of *human* and *horse*.

فائدةٌ [تقسيمُ الكليّاتِ إلى الذاتيّاتِ والعرضيّاتِ]

وإذْ قـد علمـتَ بمـا ذكرنا أنَّ الكليّاتِ خمـسٌ - الأوّلُ: الجنسُ، والثاني: النوعُ، والثالثُ: الفصلُ، والرابعُ: الخاصّةُ، والخامسُ: العَرَضُ العامُّ - فاعلمْ أنَّ الثلاثةَ الأوّلَ يُقالُ لها: «الذاتيّاتُ»، ويُقالَ للآخرينَ: «العَرَضيّاتِ». وقد يُختصُّ اسمُ ا«لذاتيِّ» بالجنسِ والفصلِ فقطْ، ولا يُطلقُ على النوعِ بهذا الإطلاقِ لفظُ «الذاتيِّ». (د٩٠)

Now that you know what we mentioned – that the universals are five:

1. genus (*jins*),
2. species (*nawʿ*),

3. differentia (*faṣl*),
4. proprium (*khāṣṣah*), and
5. general accident (*ʿaraḍ ʿāmm*)

– know that the first three are referred to as *essentials* (*dhātiyyāt*) and the other two as *accidentals* (*ʿaraḍiyyāt*).

The noun *essential* can be restricted to just the genus and differentia, in which case the term *essential* is not applied to species in an unqualified manner.

فصلٌ [أقسامُ العَرَضيّاتِ]

العرضـيُّ - أعنـي: الخاصّـةَ والعَرَضَ العـامَّ - ينقسـمُ إلـىٰ: لازمٍ ومفارقٍ. (ب٤٠)

The accident (*ʿaraḍī*) – meaning both the proprium and the general accident – is divided into inseparable (*lāzim*) and separable (*mufāriq*).

فـاللازمُ مـا يمتنـعُ انفكاكُه عن الشـيءِ، إمّـا بالنظرِ إلى الماهيّةِ كالزوجيّةِ للأربعةِ، والفرديّةِ للثلاثة، فإنَّ انفـكاكَ الزوجيّةِ عن الأربعةِ والفرديّةِ عن الثلاثةِ مستحيلٌ.

وإمّـا بالنظرِ إلى الوجودِ كالسـوادِ للحبشـيِّ، (م٢٨) فإنَّ انفكاكَ السـوادِ عـن وجـودِ الحبشـيِّ مسـتحيلٌ لا عـن ماهيّتِـه؛ لأنَّ ماهيّتَه الإنسانُ، والسوادُ ليسَ بلازمٍ للإنسانِ.

An *inseparable accident* (*ʿaraḍ lāzim*) is one that is impossible to detach from the entity, either with respect to its quiddity (*māhiyyah*) – such as evenness for four and oddness for three, since separating evenness from four and oddness from three is impossible – or with respect to existence, such as blackness for an Ethiopian (*ḥabashī*), since detaching blackness from the existence of an Ethiopian is impossible, though not from his quiddity, since his quiddity is human and blackness is not an inseparable accident for human.

والعَـرَضُ المفـارقُ: مـا لم يمتنـعْ انفكاكُه عن الملـزومٍ، كالكتابةِ بالفعلِ للإنسانِ، والمشي بالفعلِ له.

A *separable accident* ('*araḍ mufāriq*) is one that is not impossible to detach from its subject, such as *writing* or *walking* for a human.

<table>
<tr><td>

INSEPARABLE ACCIDENTS

</td><td>

فصلٌ [أقسامُ العرضيِّ اللازمِ]

</td></tr>
</table>

العَرَضُ اللازمُ قسمانِ. ‹د٩١›

Inseparable accidents are divided into two categories.

الأوّلُ: ما يلزمُ تصوّرُه مِن تصوّرِ الملزومٍ، كالبصر للعمىٰ.

The first [*al-lāzim al-bayyin bi-l-ma'nā al-akhaṣṣ, inseparable accident in the restricted sense*] is that whose apprehension necessitates apprehending what it attaches to. Such as *sight* for *blindness*.

والثانـي: مـا يلزمُ مِن تصوّرِ الملزومٍ واللازمِ الجزمُ باللزومِ، كالزوجيّةِ للأربعـةِ؛ فإنَّ مَـن تصوّرَ الأربعةَ وتصـوّرَ مفهومَ الزوجيّةِ يجزمُ بداهةً أنَّ الأربعةَ زوجٌ، ومنقسمةٌ بمتساويينِ كاملينِ.

The second [*al-lāzim al-bayyin bi-l-ma'nā al-a'amm, inseparable accident in the more general sense*] is that whose apprehension of the inseparable accident and what it attaches to necessitates certitude in the inseparability. Such as whoever apprehends *four* and apprehends the concept of evenness is immediately certain that four is even and divides into two whole equal parts.

فصلٌ [أقسامُ العرضيِّ المفارقِ]

العَـرَضُ المفارقُ، أعني: ما يمكـنُ انفكاكُه عن المعروضِ، أيضًا قسمانِ.

Separable accidents (i.e. what can be detached from its accident-recipient), are also divided into two categories.

أحدُهما: ما يدومُ عروضُه للملزومِ، كالحركةِ للفلكِ.

The first is that which remains for whatever it attaches to. Such as motion for celestial bodies.

والثاني: ما يزولُ عنه، إمّا بسرعةٍ، كحمرةِ الخجلِ، وصفرةِ الوجلِ، وإمّا ببطءٍ، كالشيبِ، والشبابِ. ‹ب٤١›

The second is that which abates from it [what it attaches to], either quickly (such as the blush of shame and the pallor of fear), or slowly (such as grey hair and youth).

فصلٌ: في التعريفاتِ

معرِّفُ الشيءِ ما يُحملُ عليه لإفادةِ تصوّرِه. ‹د٩٢› وهو علىٰ أربعةِ أقسامٍ: ١- الحدُّ التامُّ، ٢- والحدُّ الناقصُ، ٣- والرسمُ التامُّ، ٤- والرسمُ الناقصُ. ‹ب٤٢›

A thing's *definiens* (*mu'arrif*) is what is predicated of it to convey its conception. It is divided into four types:
1. The complete true definition (*ḥadd tāmm*).
2. The incomplete true definition (*ḥadd nāqiṣ*).
3. The complete descriptive definition (*rasm tāmm*).
4. The incomplete descriptive definition (*rasm nāqiṣ*).

فالتعريفُ إنْ كانَ ﴿م٢٩﴾ بالجنسِ القريبِ والفصلِ القريبِ يُسمّىٰ:
«حدًّا تامًّا»، كتعريفِ الإنسانِ بالحيوانِ الناطقِ.

If the definition is made with the proximate genus and the proximate differentia, it is called a *complete true definition* (*ḥadd tāmm*).

For example, defining *human* as *rational animal.*

وإنْ كانَ بالجنـسِ البعيـدِ والفصـلِ القريـبِ أو بـه وحدَه يُسـمّىٰ:
«حدًّا ناقصًا».

If it is made with the remote genus and the proximate differentia, or with the differentia alone, it is called an *incomplete true definition* (*ḥadd nāqiṣ*).

وإنْ كانَ بالجنسِ القريبِ والخاصّةِ يُسمّىٰ: «رسمًا تامًّا».

If it is made with the proximate genus and proprium, it is called a *complete descriptive definition* (*rasm tāmm*).

وإنْ كانَ بالجنـسِ البعيـدِ والخاصّـةِ، أو ﴿د٣٩﴾ بالخاصّـةِ وحدَهـا
يُسمّىٰ: «رسمًا ناقصًا».

If it is made with the remote genus and proprium, or the proprium alone, it is called an *incomplete descriptive definition* (*rasm nāqiṣ*).

مثالُ الحدِّ الناقصِ: تعريفُ الإنسانِ بالجسمِ الناطقِ، أو بالناطقِ فقطْ.

An example of an incomplete true definition is defining *human* as *rational body* or simply as *rational.*

ومثالُ الرسمِ التامِّ: تعريفُ الإنسانِ بالحيوانِ الضاحكِ.

An example of a complete descriptive definition is defining *human* as *laughing animal.*

ومثـال الرسـمِ الناقصِ: تعريفُه بالجسـمِ الضاحـكِ، أو بالضاحكِ
وحدَه.

An example of an incomplete descriptive definition is defining *human* as *laughing body* or simply as *laughing*.

ولا دخلَ في التعريفاتِ للعرضِ العامِّ؛ لأنَّه لا يفيدُ التمييزَ. (م ٣٠)

The general accident has no role in definitions, since it does not serve to differentiate.

<table><tr><td>TYPES OF DEFINITION</td><td>فصلٌ [في أقسام التعريف]</td></tr></table>

التعريفُ قد يكونُ حقيقيًّا، كما ذكرنا.

A definition can be *proper* (*ḥaqīqī*), as we have mentioned earlier.

وقد يكونُ لفظيًّا، وهو: ما يُقصدُ به تفسيرُ مدلولِ اللفظِ، كقولِهم:
«سعدانةٌ نبتٌ»، و «الغَضَنْفَرُ الأسدُ».

It can also be *verbal* (*lafẓī*), which is a definition intended to explain the indication of an expression. For example, their statement: "*Saʿdānah* is a plant" or "*Ghaḍanfar* is a lion."

***

وهاهنا قد تمَّ بحثُ التصوّراتِ، أعني: القولَ الشارحَ. (ب ٤٣، د ٩٤)

At this point, we have completed the discussion of conceptions, i.e. the explanatory statement (*qawl shāriḥ*).

ARGUMENTATION AND RELATED MATTERS

البابُ الثاني: في الحجّةِ وما يتعلّقُ بها

البابُ الثاني: في الحجّةِ وما يتعلّقُ بها

PROPOSITIONS

فصلٌ: في القضايا

«القضيّةُ»: قولٌ يحتملُ الصدقُ والكذبُ. وقيلَ: قولٌ يُقالُ لقائلِه إنَّه صادقٌ أو كاذبٌ.

A *proposition* (qaḍiyyah) is a statement that is conceivable to be true or false.

It is also said: A [proposition is a] statement whose speaker is said to be truthful or lying.

وهي قسمانِ: حمليّةٌ، وشرطيّةٌ.

There are two types of propositions: *predicating* and *conditional*.

أمّـا الحمليّـةُ، فهـي: ما حُكِمَ فيها بثبوتِ شـيءٍ لشيءٍ، أو نفيه عنه، كقولِكَ: «زيدٌ قائمٌ»، و «زيدٌ ليسَ بقائمٍ».

A *predicating proposition* (ḥamliyyah) is one wherein it is asserted that one thing is affirmed for another or negated from it. Such as your statement: "Zaid is standing" or "Zaid is not standing."[25]

---

25 (Tr:) Underlines have been added to predicating propositions beneath their subject and predicate to assist readers in identifying the major parts.

وَأَمَّا الشرطيّةُ: فما لا يكونُ فيه ذلكَ الحكمُ.

A *conditional proposition* (*sharṭiyyah*) is one which does not contain that judgement.

وَقِيلَ: الشرطيّةُ ما تنحلُّ إلى قضيّتَينِ، كقولِكَ: «إنْ كانتْ (م٣١) الشـمسُ طالعةً فالنهارُ موجودٌ»، (د٩٥)، و «ليسَ البتّةَ إذا كانتْ الشمسُ طالعةً فالليلُ موجودٌ». فإذا حذفتَ الأدواتِ بقي: «الشمسُ طالعةٌ، والنهارُ موجودٌ». (ب٤٤)

والحمليّـةُ مـا لا تنحلُّ إلى قضيّتَينِ، بل تنحلُّ: إمّـا إلى مفردينِ كقولِكَ: «زيدٌ هو قائمٌ»؛ فإنَّكَ إذا حذفتَ الرابطةَ أعني: «هو»، بقي لـكَ «زيـدٌ» و «قائمٌ»، وهما مفردانِ. وإمّـا إلى مفردٍ وقضيّةٍ، كما في قولِـكَ: «زيـدٌ أبـوه قائمٌ»، فإذا حللتَه بقي: «زيدٌ» وهو مفردٌ، و «أبوه قائمٌ» وهو فضيّةٌ.

It is said that (1) a *conditional proposition* (*al-qaḍiyyah al-sharṭi-yyah*) is what can be decomposed into two propositions. Such as your statements "If the sun is risen, then daytime is present" and "It is never at all that when the sun is risen that nighttime is present." When you remove the operands (*adawāt*, pl. of *ādah*), what remains are "The sun is risen" and "Daytime is present."

And (2) a *predicating proposition* (*al-qaḍiyyah al-ḥamliyyah*) is what cannot be decomposed into two propositions. Instead, it can be decomposed either into (a) two simple expressions (such as your statement: "Zaid is the one standing," for if you remove the copula [i.e. "the one"], you are left with "Zaid" and "standing," which are two simple expressions), or (b) a simple expression and a proposition (such as your statement: "Zaid: his father standing," for if you decompose it, what remains is "Zaid," which is a simple expression, and "his father standing," which is a proposition).

 فصلٌ [أقسامُ القضيّةِ الحمليّةِ]

الحمليّةُ ضربانِ.

«موجبةٌ»: وهي التي حُكِمَ فيها بثبوتِ شيءٍ لشيءٍ.

«وسالبةٌ»: وهي التي حُكِمَ فيها بنفيِ شيءٍ عن شيءٍ.

نحوُ: «الإنسانُ حيوانٌ»، و«الإنسانُ ليسَ بفرسٍ».

Predicating propositions are of two types.

(1) *Affirmative* (*mūjabah*) is one wherein it is asserted that something is affirmed for something else.

(2) *Negative* (*sālibah*) is one wherein it is asserted that something is negated from something else.

For example: "Humans are animals" and "Humans are not horses."

COMPONENTS OF PREDICATING PROPOSITIONS   فصلٌ [أجزاءُ القضيّةِ الحمليّةِ]

الحمليّةُ تلتئمُ مِن أجزاءٍ ثلاثةٍ.

أحدُها: المحكومُ عليه، (د٩٦) ويُسمّىٰ «موضوعًا».

والثاني: المحكومُ به، ويُسمّىٰ «محمولًا».

والثالث: الدالُّ على الرابطِ، ويُسمّىٰ «الرابطةَ». (ب٤٥)

A predicating proposition consists of three components.

The first component is the recipient of the judgement, called the *subject*.

The second is that which is judged, called the *predicate*.

The third is what indicates the connection, called the *copula*.

ففـي قولِـكَ: «زيــدٌ هــو قائمٌ»: «زيــد» محكــومٌ عليــه وموضوعٌ،
و «قائمٌ» محكومٌ به ومحمولٌ، ولفظةُ «هو» نسبةٌ ورابطةٌ.

In your statement: "Zaid is standing": "Zaid" is the subject,
"standing" is the predicate, and the word "is" is a relation and
the copula.[26]

وقد تُحذفُ الرابطةُ في اللفظِ دونَ المرادِ، فيُقالُ: «زيدٌ قائمٌ». ‹م ٣٢›

The copula can be omitted from the expression without changing the intended meaning,[27] so you can also say "Zaid [is] standing."

COMPONENTS OF CONDITIONAL
PROPOSITIONS

فصلٌ [أجزاءُ القضيّةِ الشرطيّةِ]

للشرطيّةِ أيضًا أجزاءٌ، ويُسمّى الجزءُ الأوّلُ مِنْها: «مقدَّما»، والجزءُ
الثاني مِنْها: «تاليًا».

A conditional proposition also has components.
The first part of it is called the *antecedent* (*muqaddam*).
The second part of it is called the *consequent* (*tālī*).

ففي قولِكَ: «إنْ كانتْ الشمسُ طالعةً كانَ النهارُ موجودًا»: قولُك:
«إنْ كانتْ الشمسُ طالعةً» مقدَّمٌ، وقولُكَ: «كانَ النهارُ موجودًا» تالٍ،
والرابطةُ هي الحكمُ بينَهما. ‹د ٩٧›

In your statement: "If the sun is risen, then it is daytime," your
statement: "If the sun is risen" is the antecedent, your statement:
"it is daytime" is the consequent, and the copula is the judgement
between them.

---

26 (Tr:) Readers of Arabic should refer to the Arabic original here, as there is
    more going on in Arabic.

27 (Tr:) This is true for some languages, such as Arabic. But some languages
    require an explicit copula. And that is why the following example requires
    bringing back the copula: "[is]".

فصلٌ [تقسيمُ القضيّةِ باعتبارِ الموضوعِ]

قد تُقسمُ القضيّةُ باعتبارِ الموضوعِ.

The proposition can be divided based on its subject.

فالموضوعُ إنْ كانَ جزئيًّا وشخصًا معيَّنًا سُمّيت القضيّةُ: «شخصيّة» و«مخصوصةً»، كقولِكَ: «زيدٌ قائمٌ».

If the subject is a particular or a specified individual, the proposition is called *personal* (*shakhṣiyyah*, lit. personal) or *exclusive* (*makhṣūṣah*). Such as your statement: "Zaid is standing."

وإنْ لم يكنْ جزئيًّا بل كانَ كلّيًّا ‹م٣٣› فهو على أنحاءٍ لأنَّها...

If the subject is not specific, but rather universal, it has several varieties since:

إنْ كانَ الحكمُ فيها على نفسِ الحقيقةِ تُسمّى القضيّةُ: «طبيعيّةً»، نحوُ: «الإنسانُ نوعٌ»، و«الحيوانُ جنسٌ».

(1) If the judgement is made about the subject's reality (*ḥaqīqah*), the proposition is called *natural* (*ṭabʿiyyah*). For example: "Human is a species" and "Animal is a genus."

وإنْ كانَ على أفرادِها فلا يخلو: ‹ب٤٦› إمّا أنْ تكونَ كمّيّةُ الأفرادِ فيها مُبيَّنتًا، أو لم تكنْ.

(2) If it is made about its members, then it is not without the possibility that either the quantity of its members is explicit, or not.

فإن بُيِّنَتْ كمّيّةُ الأفرادِ تُسمّى القضيّةُ: «محصورةً»، كقولِكَ: «كلُّ إنسانٍ حيوانٌ»، أو «بعضُ الحيوانِ إنسانٌ».

(2a) If the number of members is explicit, the proposition is called *bounded* (*maḥṣūrah*).[28] For example: "All humans are animals" or "Some animals are humans."

وإنْ لـمْ تُبَيَّـنْ تُسـمّى القضيّـة «مهملـةً»، نحـو: «الإنسـانُ في خسرٍ». (د٩٨)

(2b) If it is not explicit, the proposition is called *indeterminate* (*muhmalah*). For example: "Humans are in loss."

فصلٌ [القضايا المحصورةُ]

BOUNDED PROPOSITIONS

المحصوراتُ أربعٌ.

Bounded propositions are of four [forms].

إحداها: الموجبةُ الكلّيّةُ، كقولِكَ: «كلُّ إنسانٍ حيوانٌ».

The first is the *universal affirmative* (*al-mūjabah al-kulliyyah*). Such as your statement: "Every human is an animal."

والثانيةُ: الموجبةُ الجزئيّةُ، نحوُ: «بعضُ الحيوانِ أسودُ».

The second is the *particular affirmative* (*al-mūjabah al-juz'iyyah*). For example: "Some animals are black."

والثالثةُ: السالبةُ الكلّيّةُ، نحوُ: «لا شيءَ مِن الزنجيِّ بأبيضَ».

The third is the *universal negative* (*al-sālibah al-kulliyyah*). For example: "No black person is white."

والرابعةُ: السالبةُ الجزئيّةُ، نحوُ: «بعضُ الحيوانِ ليسَ بأسودَ».

The fourth is the *particular negative* (*al-sālibah al-juz'iyyah*). For example: "Some animals are not black."

---

28   (Tr:) "Circumscribed" is closer to the literal meaning of *maḥṣūrah*.

 فصلٌ [في أسوارِ القضايا]

الذي يبيَّنُ به كمّيّةُ الأفرادِ يُسـمّىٰ: «سـورًا»، وهو مأخوذٌ مِن سورِ البلدِ.

The term used to specify the quantity of members is called a *sūr*, derived from a territory's wall [which encloses it].

وسورُ الموجبةِ الكلّيّةِ: «كلٌّ» ولامُ الاستغراقِ. (د٩٩)

The quantifiers for universal affirmative propositions are "all" (*kull*), and the universally-inclusive definite article (*lām al-istighrāq*).

وسورُ الموجبةِ الجزئيّةِ: (م٣٤) «بعضٌ» و «واحدٌ»، نحو: «بعضٌ»

- [أ]و: «واحدٌ» - «مِن الجسمِ جمادٌ».

The quantifiers for particular affirmative propositions are "some" (*baʿḍ*) and "one." For example: "Some bodies are inanimate" and "One body is inanimate."

وسـورُ السـالبةِ الكلّيّةِ: «لا شيءَ»، و «لا واحدَ»، نحوُ: «لا شيءَ مِـن الغـرابِ بأبيـضَ»، و «لا واحدَ مِـن النارِ باردٍ». (ب٤٧) ووقوعُ النكرةِ تحتَ النفيِ نحو: «ما مِن ماءٍ إلّا وهو رطبٌ».

The quantifiers for universal negative propositions are "no" (*lā shay'*) and "not one." For example: "No crow is white" and "Not one fire is cold." The quantifier also includes the indefinite noun under negation. For example: "There is no water except that it is wet."

وسورُ السالبةِ الجزئيّةِ: «ليسَ بعضٌ»، كقولِكَ: «ليسَ بعضُ الحيوانِ بحمارٍ». و «بعضُ ليسَ»، كما تقولُ: «بعضُ الفواكةِ ليسَ بعلوٍّ».

The quantifiers for particular negative propositions are "not some" (*laysa baʿḍ*), such as your statement: "Not some of the animals are donkeys"; and "some are not" (*baʿḍ laysa*), such as your saying: "Some fruit are not elevated."

واعلمْ أنَّ في كلِّ لسانٍ سـورًا يخصُّها، ففي الفارسيّةِ لفظُ (هر)
سورُ الموجبةِ الكلّيّةِ، كقولِ الشاعرِ: (م٣٥)

Know that each language has its own quantifiers specific to it.[29] In Persian, the term "هر" (*har*) is used as the quantifier for universal affirmative propositions, such as in the poet's saying:

هر آن کس که در بندِ حرص اوفتاد * دهد خرمنِ زندگانی بباد (د١٠٠)

"Whoever falls into the shackles of greed *
gives to the wind the harvest of his life."

SOME ABBREVIATIONS EMPLOYED IN LOGIC

فصلٌ [بعضُ اختصاراتِ المناطقةِ]

قـد جـرَّتْ عادةُ الميزانيّينَ أنَّهم يعبّرونَ عن الموضوعِ بـ (ج)، وعن
المحمولِ (ب٤٨) بـ (ب).

It has become a custom for logicians to express the subject as "J" and the predicate as "B."[30]

فمتىٰ أرادوا التعبيرَ عن الموجبةِ الكلّيّةِ يقولونَ: «كلُّ ج ب».

So when they want to express a universal affirmative proposition, they say: "Every J is B."

ومرادُهم مِن ذلكَ الإيجازُ ودفعُ توهّمِ الانحصارِ.

Their intent is brevity and avoiding any misconception of limitation.[31]

---

29   (Tr:) For English, universal quantifiers include: all, everyone, any, he who, one who, whoever or whosoever, whatever or whatsoever, ever, no, none nobody. And particular quantifiers include: some, several, often, frequently, usually, sometimes, most, a few.

30   (Tr:) The convention in English texts is "S" for the subject, and "P" for the predicate.

31   (Tr:) They used symbols to emphasise the generality of form over the specificity of the oft-repeated formulaic examples.

PREDICATION

فصلٌ [في الحملِ]

الحملُ في اصطلاحِهـم: اتّحادُ المتغايرينِ في المفهومِ بحسـبِ الوجودِ، ففـي قولِـكَ: (د ١٠١) «زيـدٌ كاتـبٌ، وعمرُو شاعرٌ» مفهومُ «زيـدٌ» مغايرٌ لمفهـومِ «كاتبٍ»، لكنَّهما موجودانِ بوجودٍ (م ٣٦) واحدٍ وكذا مفهومُ «عمرٍو» و «شاعرٍ» متغايرٌ وقد اتّحدا في الوجودِ.

Predication (ḥaml), in their terminology, is the unification of two distinct concepts in meaning with respect to existence.[32] In your statements, "Zaid is a writer" and "'Amr is a poet," the concept of *Zaid* is distinct from the concept of *writer*, yet both exist in a single existence. Likewise, the concepts of *'Amr* and *poet* are distinct but united in existence.

ثـمَّ الحمـلُ علىٰ قسـمينِ؛ لأنَّه إنْ كانَ بواسـطةٍ «في» أو «ذو» أو «اللامِ» كما في قولِكَ: «زيدٌ في الدارِ»، و «المالُ لزيدٍ»، و «خالدٌ ذو مـالٍ» يُسـمّىٰ: «الحمـلُ بالاشـتقاقِ». وإنْ لم يكـنْ كذلكَ، بل يُحملُ شـيءٌ علىٰ شـيءٍ بلا واسطةِ هذهِ الوسـائطِ (ب ٤٩) يُقالُ له: «الحملُ بالمواطأةِ»، نحوُ: «عمرٌو طبيبٌ»، و «بكرٌ فصيحٌ». (د ١٠٢)

Then, predication is of two types. If it occurs through an intermediary such as "in" (*fī*), "possessor of" (*dhū*), or "belongs to" (*lām*) – as in: "Zaid is in the house," "The money is possessed by Zaid," and "Khaled is the possessor of wealth" – it is called *predication by derivation* (ḥaml bi-l-ishtiqāq). If it does not occur in that manner, and instead something is predicated of another without any intermediary of these particles, it is called *predication by equipollence* (ḥaml bi-l-muwāṭaʾah), such as "'Amr is a doctor" and "Bakr is eloquent."

---

32   An affirmative predication between two things requires the subject and predicate being united in quiddity (huwiyyah) and existence for it to be valid. Cf. al-Bushrā edition, 49.

ANOTHER DIVISION OF THE PREDICATING PROPOSITION

فصلٌ: تقسيمٌ آخرُ للحمليّةِ

موضـوعُ الحمليّـةِ إنْ كانَ موجودًا في الخـارجِ، وكانَ الحكمُ فيها باعتبـارِ تحقّقِ الموضوعِ ووجودِه في الخـارجِ كانتِ القضيّةُ خارجيّةً، نحو: «الإنسانُ كاتبٌ».

If the subject of the predicating proposition exists in external actuality (*fi-l-khārij*) and the associated judgement is made considering the subject's actual extra-mental existence, the proposition is *external* (*khārijiyyah*) – such as "The human is a writer."

وإنْ كانَ موجـودًا فـي الذهنِ، وكانَ الحكـمُ بخصوصٍ وجودِه في الذهنِ كانتْ «ذهنيّةً»، نحو: «الإنسانُ كلّيٌّ».

If the subject exists within the mind, and the judgement pertains specifically to its mind-dependent existence, it is called *mental* (*dhihniyyah*) – such as "Human is a universal."

وإنْ كانَ الحكـمُ باعتبـارِ تقـرّرِه في الواقـعِ مـع عـزلِ النظـرِ عن خصوصيّةٍ ظرفِ الخارجِ أو الذهنِ سُمّيتْ القضيّةُ: «حقيقيّةٌ»، نحو: «الأربعةُ زوجٌ»، و «الستّةُ ضعفُ الثلاثةِ». (م٣٧، ب٥٠، د١٠٣)

If the judgement is made based on the subject's occurrence in reality while abstracting from the particular circumstances of its being extra-mental or mind-dependent, then it is called *veridical* (*ḥaqīqiyyah*) – such as "Four is even." and "Six is twice that of three."

ANOTHER DIVISION OF THE PROPOSITION

فصلٌ [تقسيمٌ آخرُ للقضيّةِ]

القضيّةُ الموجبةُ وكذا السالبةُ تنقسمانِ إلىٰ: معدولةٍ وغيرِ معدولةٍ.

An affirmative proposition, as well as a negative one, is divided into *oblique* (*ma'dūlah*) and *non-oblique* (*ghayr ma'dūlah*).

فالمعدولةُ: مـا يكونُ فيها حرفُ السـلبِ جزءًا مِن الموضوعِ، أو مِن المحمولِ، أو كِلَّيهما، مثالُ الأوَّلِ قولُنا: «اللاحيّ جمادٌ»، ومثالُ الثانـي: «زيـدٌ لا عالمٌ»، ومثالُ الثالـثِ: «اللاحيّ لا عالمٌ»، هذا في الإيجابِ.

An *oblique proposition* (*ma'dūlah*) is one in which the particle of negation is part of the subject, the predicate, or both. An example of the first is our statement: "The non-living is inanimate"; an example of the second is: "Zaid is not knowledgeable"; and an example of the third is: "The non-living is not knowledgeable." This applies to affirmative propositions.

أمّا في السلبِ فمثالُ الأوَّلِ: «اللاحي ليسَ بعالمٍ»، ومثالُ الثاني: «العالمُ ليسَ بلاحيّ»، ومثالُ الثالثِ: «اللاحيّ ليسَ بلا جمادٍ».

As for negative propositions, an example of the first is: "The non-living is not knowledgeable"; an example of the second is: "The knowledgeable is not non-living"; and an example of the third is: "The non-living is not devoid of being inanimate."

وغيرُ المعدولةِ: بخلافِها، وتُسـمَّى [33] غيرُ المعدولة في الموجبةِ بـ «المحصَّلةِ»، وفي السالبةِ بـ «البسيطةِ».

A *non-oblique proposition* (*ghayr ma'dūlah*) is the opposite of this. It is called *straightforward* (*muḥaṣṣalah*) in the affirmative and *simple* (*basīṭah*) in the negative.

33　Dār al-Mālik edition: (تسمى); Dār al-Nūr edition: (يسمّى). The feminine form is grammatically preferable given the feminine referent.

MODAL PROPOSITIONS

فصلٌ [القضايا الموجّهةِ]

قـد تُذكَـرُ الجهـةُ في القضيّـةِ فتُسـمّىٰ: «موجّهـةً»، و «رباعيّةً» أيضًا. (ب١٥)

The mode (*jihah*) may be mentioned in the proposition, in which case it is called a *modal proposition* (*muwajjahah*), and it is a *fourfold* (*rubā'iyyah*).

والموجّهاتُ خمسـةَ عشـرَ، (د١٠٤) ثمانيةٌ مِنْها بسـيطةٌ، وسـبعةٌ مِنْها مركّبةٌ.

Modal propositions are fifteen in total: eight of them are simple (*basīṭah*), while seven are compound (*murakkabah*).

SIMPLE MODAL PROPOSITIONS

[البسائط]

أمّا البسائطُ، فإحداها: الضروريّةُ المطلقةُ، (م٣٨) وهي: التي حُكِمَ فيهـا بضـرورةِ ثبوتِ المحمولِ للموضوعِ أو سلبِه عنه، ما دامتْ ذاتُ الموضوعِ موجودةً، كقولِكَ: «الإنسانُ حيوانٌ بالضرورةِ»، و «الإنسانُ ليسَ بحجرٍ بالضرورةِ».

As for the *simple modal propositions* (*basīṭah*), the first is the *absolute necessity* (*ḍarūriyyah muṭlaqah*): the proposition in which the necessity of affirming or denying the predicate in relation to the subject is judged for as long as the entity of the subject exists – such as "Humans are animals, necessarily" and "Humans are not stones, necessarily."

والثانيةُ: الدائمـةُ المطلقةُ، (د١٠٥) وهي: التـي حُكِمَ فيها بدوامِ ثبوتِ المحمولِ للموضوعِ أو سـلبِه عنه، كقولِكَ: «كلُّ فلكٍ متحرّكٌ بالدوامِ»، و «لا شيءَ مِن الفلكِ بساكنٍ بالدوامِ». (ب٢٥)

The second is the *absolute perpetuity* (*dā'imah muṭlaqah*): a proposition in which the perpetual affirmation or negation of the predicate in relation to the subject is judged – such as "Every celestial body is moving, always" and "No celestial body is stationary, always."

والثالثـةُ: المشـروطةُ العامّةُ، وهي: التي حُكِـمَ فيها بضرورةِ ثبوتِ المحمـولِ للموضوعِ أو نفيـه عنه مـا دامتْ ذاتُ الموضوعِ موصوفةً بالوصفِ العنوانيِّ. والوصفُ العنوانيُّ عندَهم: ما عُبِّرَ به عن الموضوعِ، كقولِنـا: «كلُّ كاتبٍ متحرّكُ الأصابع بالضرورةِ ما دامَ كاتبًا»، و«لا شيءَ مِن (٣٩م) الكاتبِ بساكنِ الأصابعِ بالضرورةِ ما دامَ كاتبًا».

The third is the *general conditional* (*mashrūṭah 'āmmah*): a proposition in which the necessity of affirming or denying the predicate in relation to the subject is judged for as long as the subject remains described by its *defining characteristic* (*waṣf 'unwānī*).

According to them, the *defining characteristic* (*waṣf 'unwānī*) is that which is used to designate the subject – such as "Every writer has moving fingers, necessarily, for as long as he is a writer" and "No writer has stationary fingers, necessarily, for as long as he is a writer."

والرابعةُ: العرفيّةُ العامّةُ، وهي: التي حُكِمَ فيها بدوامِ ثبوتِ المحمولِ للموضوعِ، أو سـلبِه عنه، ما دامـتْ ذاتُ الموضوعِ متّصفةً بالوصفِ العنوانيِّ، كقولِنا: «بالدوامِ كلُّ كاتبٍ متحرّكُ الأصابعِ ما دامَ كاتبًا»، و«بالدوامِ لا شيءَ مِن النائمِ مستيقظٌ ما دامَ نائمًا». (د١٠٦)

The fourth is the *general customary* (*'urfiyyah 'āmmah*): a proposition in which the perpetual affirmation or negation of the predicate in relation to the subject is judged for as long as the subject remains described by its defining characteristic (*waṣf 'unwānī*, lit. titular description) – such as "Always, every writer has moving fingers, for as long as he is a writer" and "Always, no sleeper is awake, for as long as he is asleep."

والخامسةُ: الوقتيّةُ المطلقةُ، وهي: التي حُكِمَ فيها بثبوتِ المحمولِ للموضــوعِ، أو نفيـه عنـه، فـي وقتٍ مِـن أوقاتِ الـذاتِ، كما تقولُ: «كلُّ قمرٍ منخسفٍ بالضرورةِ وقتَ حيلولةِ الأرضِ بينَه وبينَ ‹ب٥٣› الشمسِ»، و «لا شيءَ مِن القمرِ بمنخسفٍ بالضرورةِ وقتَ التربيعِ».

The fifth is the *absolute temporal* (waqtiyyah muṭlaqah): a proposition in which the affirmation or negation of the predicate in relation to the subject is judged at a specific time within the subject's existence – such as "Every moon is eclipsed, necessarily, at the time when the Earth comes between it and the sun" and "No moon is eclipsed, necessarily, at the time of the quadrature."[34]

والسادسـةُ: المنتشـرةُ المطلقـةُ، وهي: التـي حُكِمَ فيهـا بثبوتِ المحمـولِ للموضـوعِ، أو نفيـه عنـه، فـي وقتٍ غيرِ معيّنٍ مِـن أوقاتِ الذاتِ، نحوُ: «كلُّ حيوانٍ متنفّسٌ بالضرورةِ وقتًا ما»، و «لا شيءَ مِن الحجرِ بمتنفّسٍ بالضرورةِ وقتًا ما».

The sixth is the *absolute scattered* (muntasharah muṭlaqah): a proposition in which the affirmation or negation of the predicate in relation to the subject is judged at an unspecified time within the subject's existence – such as "Every living creature is breathing, necessarily, at some time" and "No stone is breathing, necessarily, at some time."

والسابعةُ: المطلقةُ العامّةُ، وهي: التي حُكِمَ فيها بوجودِ المحمولِ للموضوعِ، أو سلبِه عنه، أي: في أحدِ الأزمنةِ الثلاثةِ، كقولِكَ: «كلُّ

---

34   (Tr:) The position of the moon or a planet when it is 90° from the sun as viewed from the earth.

إنسانٍ ضاحكٌ بالفعلِ»»، و «لا شيءَ مِن الإنسانِ بضاحكٍ بالفعلِ».

(د٨٠١)

The seventh is the *general absolute (muṭlaqah ʿāmmah)*: a proposition in which the existence or non-existence of the predicate in relation to the subject is judged at some point in one of the three time periods [past, present, and future] – such as "Every human is laughing, actually" and "No human is laughing, actually."

والثامنةُ: الممكنـةُ العامّـةُ، وهي: التي حُكِمَ فيها بسـلبِ ضرورةِ الجانـبِ المخالـفِ، كقولِكَ: «كلُّ نارٍ حارّةٌ بالإمكانِ العامّ»، و «لا شيءَ مِن النارِ بباردةٍ بالإمكانِ العامّ». (م٠٤، ب٤٥)

The eighth is *general possibility (al-mumkinah al-ʿāmmah)*: a proposition in which necessity is negated from the opposing side[35] – such as "Every fire is hot, possibly" and "No fire is cold, possibly."[36]

COMPOUND [MODAL] PROPOSITIONS فصلٌ: في المركّباتِ

المركّبةُ: قضيّةٌ رُكِّبَتْ حقيقتُها مِن إيجابٍ وسلبٍ.

A *compound modal proposition (murakkab)* is one whose true nature (*ḥaqīqah*) is composed of both an affirmation and a negation.

---

35   (Tr:) Opposing side here refers to affirmation or negation. Allowing for possibility naturally follows from their negation.

36   If negating heat from fire were necessary, the affirmative would not be valid. Likewise, if the affirmative were required, it would not be valid to negate coldness from fire, necessarily. It is named "possibility" because it being possible to affirm the predicate to the subject, or to negate it from it. It is named "general" because it is more general than special possibility, which will come in compound modals. C.f. Sālim, *Taysīr al-qawāʿid al-manṭiqiyyah*, 126.

والاعتبارُ في تسميتِها «موجبةً» أو «سالبةً» للجزءِ الأوَّلِ.

In naming it as affirmative (*mūjabah*) or negative (*sālibah*), consideration is given to the first part of the proposition.

فإنْ كانَ الجزءُ الأوَّلُ موجبًا كقولِكَ: «بالضرورةِ كلُّ كاتبٍ متحرِّكُ الأصابعِ ما دامَ كاتبًا لا دائمًا»، سُمِّيتْ: «موجبةً».

If the first part is affirmative – such as "Necessarily, every writer has moving fingers, for as long as he is a writer, but not always" – then it is called *affirmative* (*mūjabah*).

وإنْ كانَ الجزءُ الأوَّلُ سالبًا كقولِنا: «بالضرورةِ لا شيءَ مِن الكاتبِ بساكنِ الأصابعِ ما دامَ كاتبًا لا دائمًا»، سُمِّيتْ: «سالبةً». (د١٠٨)

If the first part is negative – such as "Necessarily, no writer has stationary fingers, for as long as he is a writer, but not always" – then it is called *negative* (*sālibah*).

ومِن المركّباتِ: المشروطةُ الخاصّةُ، وهي: المشروطةُ العامّةُ مع قيدِ اللادوامِ بحسبِ الذاتِ، ومرَّ مثالُها إيجابًا وسلبًا.

Among the compound modal propositions (*murakkabah*) is the *special conditional* (*mashrūṭah khāṣṣah*): a general conditional proposition restricted by non-perpetuity with respect to the entity.

Its affirmative and negative examples have already been mentioned.

ومِنهـا: العرفيّةُ الخاصّةُ، وهـي: العرفيّةُ العامّةُ مع قيدِ اللادوامِ بحسـبِ الـذاتِ، كمـا تقولُ: «دائمًا كلُّ كاتبٍ متحرِّكُ الأصابعِ ما دامَ كلُّ كاتبٍ كاتبًا لا دائمًا»، و«دائمًا لا شيءَ مِن الكاتبِ بساكنِ الأصابعِ ما دامَ كاتبًا لا دائمًا».

Among them is the *special customary* (*'urfiyyah khāṣṣah*): a general customary proposition restricted by non-perpetuity with respect to the entity – such as "Always, every writer has moving fingers, for as long as every writer is a writer, but not always" and "Always, no writer has stationary fingers, for as long as he is a writer, but not always."

ومِنْها: الوجوديّةُ اللاضروريّةُ، (ب٥٥) وهي: المطلقةُ العامّةُ مع قيدِ اللاضرورةِ بحسبِ الذاتِ، (م٤١) كقولِنا: «كلُّ إنسانٍ كاتبٌ بالفعلِ لا بالضرورةِ» في الإيجابِ، و«لا شيءَ مِن الإنسانِ بكاتبٍ بالفعلِ لا بالضرورةِ» في السلبِ.

Among them is the *non-necessary existential* (*wujūdiyyah lāḍarūriyyah*): a general absolute proposition restricted by non-necessity with respect to the entity – such as "Every person is a writer, actually, but not necessarily" (*in the affirmative*) and "No human is a writer, actually, but not necessarily" (*n the negative*).

ومِنْها: الوجوديّةُ اللادائمةُ، وهي: المطلقةُ العامّةُ مع اللادوامِ بحسبِ الذاتِ، كقولِكَ في الإيجابِ: «كلُّ إنسانٍ ضاحكٌ بالفعلِ لا دائمًا»، وقولِكَ [في السلبِ]: «لا شيءَ مِن الإنسانِ بضاحكٍ بالفعلِ لا دائمًا». (د١٠٩)

Among them is the *non-perpetual existential* (*wujūdiyyah lādā'imah*): a general absolute proposition restricted by non-perpetuity with respect to the entity – such as "Every person is laughing, actually, but not always" (*in the affirmative*) and "No human is laughing, actually, but not always" (*in the negative*).

ومِنْها: الوقتيّةُ، وهي: الوقتيّةُ المطلقةُ إذا قُيِّدتْ باللادوامِ بحسبِ الذاتِ، كقولِنا: «بالضرورةِ كلُّ قمرٍ منخسفٍ وقتَ حيلولةِ الأرضِ

بينَه وبينَ الشـمسِ لا دائمًا»، و «لا شـيءَ مِن القمرِ بمنخسفٍ وقتَ التربيعِ لا دائمًا».

Among them is the *temporal* (*waqtiyyah*): an absolute temporal proposition when restricted by non-perpetuity with respect to the entity – such "Necessarily, every moon is eclipsed at the time the Earth comes between it and the sun, but not always" and "No moon is eclipsed at the quadrature,[37] but not always."

ومِنْهــا: المنتشــرةُ، وهـي: المنتشــرةُ المطلقـةُ المقيّـدةُ بـاللادوامِ بحسبِ الذاتِ، مثالُها: «بالضرورةِ كلُّ إنسانٍ متنفّسٌ في وقتٍ ما لا دائمًا»، و «بالضرورةِ لا شيءَ مِن الإنسانِ بمتنفّسٍ وقتًا ما لا دائمًا.

Among them is the *scattered* (*muntasharah*): an absolute scattered proposition when restricted by non-perpetuity with respect to the entity – such as "Necessarily, every human is breathing, at some time, but not always" and "Necessarily, no human is breathing, at some time, but not always."

ومِنْهــا: الممكنـةُ الخاصّةُ، وهـي: التي حُكِمَ فيها بارتفاعِ الضرورةِ المطلقةِ (ب٥٦) عـن جانبَـي الوجـودِ والعـدمِ جميعًـا، كقولِكَ: «بالإمـكانِ الخـاصِّ كلُّ إنسـانٍ ضاحكٌ»، و «بالإمـكانِ الخاصِّ لا شيءَ مِن الإنسانِ بضاحكٍ».

Among them is the *special possibility* (*mumkinah khāṣṣah*), also called two-sided possibility: a proposition in which absolute necessity is negated from both existence and non-existence simultaneously – such as "By special possibility, every human is laughing" and "By special possibility, no human is laughing."

---

37   (Tr:) The position of the moon or a planet when it is 90° from the sun as viewed from the earth.

فصلٌ [اللادوامُ واللاضرورةُ]

NON-PERPETUITY AND NON-NECESSITY

اللادوامُ إشـارةٌ إلـى مطلقـةٍ عامّـةٍ، واللاضرورةُ إلـى ممكنةٍ عامّةٍ.

(د ١١٠)

Non-perpetuity (*lā-dawām*) is an indication of a general absolute proposition, while *non-necessity* (*lā-ḍarūrah*) is an indication of a general possible proposition.

فإذا قلتَ: «كلُّ إنسانٍ متعجّبٌ بالفعلِ لا دائمًا» فكأنَّكَ قلتَ: «كلُّ إنسانٍ متعجّبٌ بالفعلِ، ولا شيءَ مِن الإنسانِ بمتعجّبٍ بالفعلِ».

Thus, if you say "Every human is amazed, actually, but not always," it is as if you said "Every human is amazed, actually, and no human is amazed, actually."

وإذا قلتَ: «كلُّ حيوانٍ ماشٍ بالفعلِ لا بالضرورةِ»، فكأنَّكَ قلتَ: «كلُّ حيوانٍ ماشٍ بالفعلِ، ولا شيءَ مِن الحيوانِ ماشٍ بالإمكانِ».

And if you say "Every animal is walking, actually, but not necessarily," it is as if you said "Every animal is walking, actually, and [at the same time,] no animal is walking, possibly."

بابُ الشرطيّةِ

CONDITIONAL PROPOSITIONS

بـابُ الشـرطيّةِ قـد عرفتَ معنى الشـرطيّةِ، وهي: التـي تنحلُّ إلـى قضيّتَينِ، والآنَ نهديكَ إلـى أقسامِها، (م٤٢) ونرشدُكَ إلى أحكامِها.

You have understood the meaning of conditional propositions, which are those that decompose into two propositions. Now, we will introduce you to their types and guide you through their rules.

فاعلــمْ أيّهــا الفَطِنُ اللبيبُ والذكي الأريبُ أنَّ الشــرطيّةَ قسـمانِ. أحدُهما: المتّصلةُ. وثانيهما المنفصلةُ. ‹٥٧ب›

Know, O discerning and intelligent one, that conditional propositions are divided into two types.

The first is the *conjunctive* (*sharṭiyyah muttaṣilah*).

The second is the *disjunctive* (*sharṭiyyah munfaṣilah*).

[تعريف الشرطيّة المتّصلة]

CONJUNCTIVE CONDITIONALS DEFINED

أمّـا المتّصلــةُ فهي: التي حُكِمَ فيها بثبوتِ نسبةٍ علىٰ تقديرِ ثبوتِ نسبةٍ أخرىٰ، في ‹١١١د› الإيجابِ، وبنفي نسبةٍ علىٰ تقديرِ نفي نسبةٍ أخـرىٰ، فــي الســلبِ. كقولِنا في الإيجابِ: «إنْ كانَ زيدٌ إنسانًا كانَ حيوانًا». وقولِنا في السلبِ: «ليسَ البتّةَ إذا كانَ زيدٌ إنسانًا كانَ فرسًا».

The *conjunctive conditional proposition* (*sharṭiyyah muttaṣilah*) is one in which it is asserted that, in the affirmative case (*ījāb*), one relation is affirmed on the condition that another relation is affirmed; and in the negative case (*salb*), one relation is negated on the condition that another relation is negated – such as, in the affirmative, "If Zaid is a human, then he is an animal," and in the negative, "It is absolutely not the case that if Zaid is a human, then he is a horse."

[أقسام الشرطيّة المتّصلة]

CONJUNCTIVE CONDITIONAL PROPOSITIONS

ثمَّ المتّصلةُ صنفانِ.

Then, the conjunctive conditional proposition (*sharṭiyyah muttaṣilah*) has two subtypes:

إنْ كانَ ذلكَ الحكمُ بعلاقةٍ بينَ المقدّمِ والتالي سُمّيتْ: «لزوميّةً»، كما مرَّ.

If the judgement establishes a *connection* (*'alāqah*) between the *antecedent* (*muqaddam*) and the *consequent* (*tālī*), it is called *implicative* (*luzūmiyyah*), as was mentioned earlier.

وإنْ كانَ ذلكَ الحكمُ بدونِ العلاقةِ سُـمِّيتْ: «اتّفاقيّةً»، كقولِكَ: (م٤٣) «إذا كانَ الإنسانُ ناطقًا فالحمارُ ناهقٌ».

If the judgement does not establish such a connection, it is called *coincidental* (*ittifāqiyyah*) – such as "If a human is rational, then a donkey is braying."

والعلاقةُ في عرفِهــم عبارةٌ عن أحدِ أمرَينِ: إمّـا أنْ يكونَ أحدُهما علّةً للآخرِ، (ب٥٨)، أو (د١١٢) كِلاهما معلولَينِ لثالثٍ. وإمّا أنْ يكونَ بينَهما علاقةُ التضايفِ.

In their terminology, *connection* (*'alāqah*) refers to one of two things: either one of them is the *cause* (*'illah*) of the other[38], or both of them are the effects of a third cause,[39] or there is an interdependent connection (*'alāqat al-taḍāyuf*) between the two.

و «التضايفُ» هــو: أنْ يكــونَ تعقّـلُ أحدِهمــا موقوفًا علــىٰ تعقّلِ الآخرِ، كالأبوّةِ والبنوّةِ.

Interdependent (*taḍāyuf*) is when the comprehension of one depends on the comprehension of the other, such as paternity and filiation.

فإذا قلتَ: «إنْ كانَ زيدٌ أبًا لعمرٍو كانَ عمرٌو ابنًا له» تكونُ شرطيّةً متّصلةً بينَ طرفَيها علاقةُ التضايفِ.

---

38 For example: "If the sun is risen, then daytime exists," since sunrise is the cause for daytime existing; and "If daytime exists, the sun is risen," since the existence of daytime is caused by the sun being risen. Cf. al-Bushrā edition, 58.

39 For example: "If the world is illuminated, daytime is present," since the world being illuminated and daytime existing are both caused by the sun being risen. Cf. al-Madīnah edition, 44 fn 3.

Thus, "If Zaid is the father of 'Amr, then 'Amr is the son of Zaid" is a conjunctive conditional proposition (*sharṭiyyah mut-taṣilah*) in which there is an interdependent connection between the two terms.

THE DISJUNCTIVE PROPOSITION DEFINED [تعريف الشرطيّةِ المنفصلةِ]

وأمّـا «المنفصلـةُ» فهـي: التي حُكِمَ فيها بالتنافي بينَ شـيئَينِ في موجبةٍ، وبسلبِ التنافي في سالبةٍ.

The disjunctive *conditional proposition* (*sharṭiyyah munfaṣilah*) is one in which it is asserted that, in the affirmative, there is an incompatibility (*tanāfur*) between two things, and, in the negative, this incompatibility is negated.

DISJUNCTIVE CONDITIONAL PROPOSITIONS   فصلٌ [أقسامُ الشرطيّةِ المنفصلةِ]

الشـرطيّةُ المنفصلـةُ علـىٰ ثلاثةِ أضـربٍ؛ لأنَّهـا إنْ^(٤٠) حُكِمَ فيها بالتنافـي أو بعدمِـه بيـنَ النسـبتَينِ فـي الصـدقِ والكذبِ معًـا كانت «المنفصلةُ حقيقيّةً»، كما تقولُ: «هذا العددُ إمّا (م ٤٤)، زوجٌ أو فردٌ»، فلا يمكنُ اجتماعُ الزوجيّةِ والفرديّةِ في عددٍ معيّنٍ، ولا ارتفاعُهما.

Disjunctive conditional propositions (*sharṭiyyah munfaṣilah*) fall into three categories, because:

1. If it is asserted that incompatibility is present or absent between the two relations in both truth and falsehood, then it is called a *genuine disjoining* (*munfaṣilah ḥaqīqiyyah*), – such as "This number is either even or odd," since evenness and oddness cannot coexist in a specific number, nor can they both be negated.

---

40   al-Madīnah edition has (إن); al-Bushrā edition does not.

وإنْ حُكِمَ بالتنافي أو بعدمِه صدقًا كانتْ «مانعةَ الجمـع»، كقولِـكَ: «هذا الشـيءُ إمّا شـجرٌ أو حجرٌ»، ‹د١١٣› فلا يمكنُ أنْ يكونَ شيءٌ معيّنٌ حجرًا وشجرًا معًا، ويمكنُ أنْ لا يكونَ شيئًا مِنهما.

2. If it is asserted that incompatibility is present or absent in truth, then it is called *excluder of conjunction* (*māni'at al-jam'*) – such as "This thing is either a tree or a stone," since a specific thing cannot be both a tree and a stone simultaneously, but it can be neither.

وإنْ حُكِمَ بالتنافي وسـلبِه كذبًا فقطْ كانتْ «مانعةَ الخلوِّ»، كقولِ القائِـلِ: «إمّـا أنْ يكونَ زيدٌ في البحرِ أو لا يغرقُ»، فارتفاعُهما بأنْ لا يكونَ زيدٌ في البحرِ ويغرقُ محالٌ، وليسَ اجتماعُهما محالا بأنْ يكونَ في البحرِ ولا يغرقُ. ‹ب٥٩›

3. If it is asserted that incompatibility is present or absent in falsehood only, then it is called *excluder of vacuity* (*māni'at al-khuluww*) – such as in someone's statement: "Either Zaid is in the sea, or he is not sinking," since their simultaneous absence (i.e. for Zaid to neither be in the sea nor sinking) is impossible, while their coexistence is not impossible (i.e. Zaid can be in the sea and also not sinking).

ANOTHER DIVISION OF THE
DISJUNCTIVE CONDITIONAL
PROPOSITION

فصلٌ [تقسيمٌ آخرُ للشرطيّةِ المنفصلةِ]

المنفصلةُ بأقسامِها الثلاثةِ قسمانِ: عناديّةٌ، واتّفاقيّةٌ.

The disjunctive conditional proposition, with its three divisions, is divided into two types: oppositional (*'inādiyyah*) and coincidental (*ittifāqiyyah*).

و «العناديّةُ»: عبارةٌ عن أنْ يكونَ فيها التنافي لذاتِهما. ‹د١١٤›

Oppositional (*'inādiyyah*) refers to the incompatibility being due to their very essence.

و «الاتّفاقيّةُ»: عبارةٌ عن أنْ يكونَ فيها التنافي بمجرّدِ الاتّفاقِ. (م٤٥)

Coincidental (*ittifāqiyyah*) refers to the incompatibility occurring merely by coincidence.

<table>
<tr><td>A THIRD DIVISION OF
CONDITIONAL PROPOSITIONS</td><td>فصلٌ [تقسيمٌ ثالثٌ للشرطيّةِ]</td></tr>
</table>

اعلــمْ أنَّــه كما تنقسـمُ الحمليّـةُ إلــىٰ: الشــخصيّةِ، والمحصورةِ، والمهملةِ، كذلكَ الشــرطيّةُ تنقسـمُ إلىٰ هذهِ الأقسـامِ، إلّا أنَّ القضيّةَ الطبيعيّةَ لا تُتصوّرُ ها هُنا.

Know that just as the predicating proposition is divided into personal, bounded, and indeterminate, the conditional proposition is also divided into these categories. However, the natural proposition is not conceivable here.

ثمَّ التقاديرُ ‹ب٦٠›، في الشرطيّةِ بمنزلةِ الأفرادِ في الحمليّةِ.

Furthermore, the *hypothetical scenarios* (*al-taqādir*)[41] in the conditional proposition have the status of members in the predicating proposition.

(١) فإنْ كانَ الحكـمُ علـىٰ تقديـرٍ معيّـنٍ ووضعٍ خاصٍّ سُــمّيت الشرطيّةُ: «شخصيّةً»، كقولِنا: «إنْ جئتَني اليومَ أكرمُكَ».

1. If the judgement is made for an identified hypothetical scenario and a specific situation, the conditional proposition is called

---

41 What is meant by "hypothetical scenarios" (*al-taqādir*) is all the circumstances that could co-occur with the Condition (*muqaddam*), even if doing so is, in itself, absurd… Cf. al-Bushrā edition, 60.

personal (*shakhṣiyyah*, lit. personal) – such as: "If you come to me today, I will honour you."

(٢) وإنْ كانَ الحكمُ على جميعِ تقاديرِ المقدّمِ سُمِّيتْ: «كُلّيّةً»، نحو: «كلّما كانتِ الشمسُ طالعةً كانَ النهارُ موجودًا».

2. If the judgement is made for all hypothetical scenarios of the antecedent, it is called *universal* (*kulliyyah*) – such as "Whenever the sun rises, it is daytime."

(٣) وإنْ كانَ الحكمُ على بعضِ التقاديرِ كانتْ «جزئيّةً»، كما في قولِنا: «قد يكونُ إذا كانَ الشيءُ حيوانًا كانَ إنسانًا».

3. If the judgement is made for some hypothetical scenarios, it is called *particular* (*juz'iyyah*) – such as: "It may be that if something is an animal, it is a human."

(٤) وإنْ تُركَ ذكرُ التقاديرِ كلًّا وبعضًا كانتْ «مهملةً»، نحو: «إنْ كانَ زيدٌ إنسانًا كانَ حيوانًا». (د١١٥)

4. If the hypothetical scenarios are omitted altogether or in part, it is called *indeterminate* (*muhmalah*) – such as "If Zaid is a human, he is an animal."

فصلٌ: في ذكرِ أسوارِ الشرطيّاتِ

سورُ الموجبةِ الكلّيّةِ في المتّصلةِ لفظُ: «متىٰ»، و «مهما»، و «كلّما»، وفي المنفصلةِ: «دائمًا».

QUANTIFIERS FOR CONDITIONAL PROPOSITIONS

The quantifiers for the universal affirmative in the conditionals (*sharṭiyyah muttaṣilah*) are "when" (*matā*), "whenever" (*mahmā*), and "every time" (*kullamā*).

And in disjunctive conditionals (*sharṭiyyah munfaṣilah*): "always" (*dā'iman*).

وسورُ السالبةِ الكلّيّةِ في المتّصلةِ والمنفصلةِ: «ليسَ البتّةَ».

The quantifier for the universal negative in both conjunctive and disjunctive conditionals is "never at all" (*laysa al-battah*).

وسورُ السالبةِ الجزئيّةِ فيهما: «قد يكونُ»، وبإدخالِ حرفِ السلبِ على سورِ الإيجابِ الكلّيِّ.

The quantifiers for the particular negative in both types are "it may be" (*qad yakūnu*), and by inserting the negative particle into the quantifier of a universal affirmative.

ولفظـةُ: «لـو» و «إن» و «إذا» فـي «ب٦١» الاتّصالِ، و «إمّا» و «أو» في الانفصالِ، تجيءُ في الإهمالِ. «م٤٦»

The expressions "if only" (*law*), "if" (*in*), and "when" (*idhā*) appear in indeterminate conjunctive conditionals, while "either" (*immā*) and "or" (*aw* appear in indeterminate disjunctive conditionals.

THE TERMS OF A CONDITIONAL
PROPOSITION
فصلٌ [في طرفَي الشرطيّةِ]

طرفَا الشرطيّةِ -أعني: المقدّمَ والتالي- لا حُكمَ فيهما حينَ كونِهما طرفَينِ، وبعدَ التحليلِ يمكنُ أنْ يعتبرَ فيهما حكمٌ.

The two terms of a conditional proposition – that is, the antecedent (*muqaddam*) and the consequent (*tālī*) – do not contain any judgement when they are considered as mere terms. However, after analysis, it is possible to consider them as containing a judgement.

فطرفاها إمّا شبيهتانِ بجملتَينِ أو متّصلتَينِ أو منفصلتَينِ أو «د١١٦» مختلفينِ.

THE TERMS OF A CONDITIONAL PROPOSITION

Its two terms can be like two independent sentences, two conjunctives, two disjunctives, or different from each other.

وعليكَ باستخراجِ الأمثلةِ. (٦٢ب)

You should extract examples for each case.[42]

---

42   Examples for the conjunctives:

1. "Whenever (*kullamā*) a thing is a human, it is an animal."

2. "Whenever (*kullamā*) if a thing is a human, then it is an animal, so whenever it is not an animal, then it is not a human."

3. "Whenever (*kullamā*) it is perpetually (*dā'imān*) that either this number is even or odd, so it is perpetually (*dā'imān*) that either it is divisible into two equals or non-divisible."

4. "If the sun's ascendance is a condition for daytime's presence, then whenever (*kullamā*) the sun is ascendent, daytime is present."

5. "If whenever (*kullamā*) the sun is ascendent, daytime is present, then the sun's ascendence is what implies (*malzūm*) daytime's presence."

6. "If this is a number, then it is perpetually (*dā'iman*) either even or odd.

7. "Whenever (*kullamā*) this is either even or odd, this is a number."

8. "If whenever (*kullamā*) the sun is ascendent, daytime is present, then perpetually (*dā'iman*) either the sun is risen and either daytime is not present."

9. "Whenever (*kullamā*) it is perpetually (*dā'iman*) either that the sun is ascendent and either that daytime is not present, then whenever (*kullamā*) the sun is ascendent, daytime is present."

Examples for the disjunctives:

1. "Either the number is even or odd."

2. "Perpetually (*dā'iman*) either if the sun is risen, then daytime is present, and either if the sun is ascendent, then daytime is not present."

3. "Always (*dā'iman*) either this number is even or odd, and either this number is non-even even and non-odd."

4. "Always (*dā'iman*) either it is not that the sun being ascendent is a cause for daytime being present; and either it is that whenever (*kullamā*) the sun is ascendent, daytime is present."

5. "Always (*dā'iman*) either it is that this thing is not a number, and either it is that it is either even or odd."

6. "Always (*dā'iman*) either it is that whenever (*kullamā*) the sun is risen, then the daytime is present; and either it is that the sun is risen, and either it is that daytime is not present."

Cf. al-Bushrā edition, 63–64.

INTRODUCTION TO THE SECTIONS ON CONTRADICTION AND CONVERSION

فصلٌ [مقدّمةُ فصولِ التناقضِ والعكوسِ]

وإذْ قـد فرغنـا مِـن بيـانِ القضايا، وذكرِ أقسـامِها الأوّليّـةِ والثانويّةِ، فحـانَ لنا أنْ نذكرَ شـيئًا مِن أحكامِها، فنقولُ مِـن أحكامِها التناقضُ والعكوسُ، فلنعقدْ لبيانِها فصولًا، ونذكرُ فيها أصولًا.

Since we have completed the explanation of propositions and their primary and secondary classifications, it is now time to discuss some of their rules. Among these rules are contradiction (*tanāquḍ*) and conversion (*'aks*).

Thus, we will arrange sections to clarify them and mention their foundational principles.

CONTRADICTION

فصلٌ [في التناقض]

«التناقـضُ» هو: اخـتلافُ القضيّتَينِ بالإيجابِ والسـلبِ، بحيثُ يقتضـي لذاتِـه صِـدقُ ‹د١١٧› إحداهمـا كذبَ الأخـرىٰ وبالعكسِ، كقولِنا: «زيدٌ قائمٌ» و «زيدٌ ليسَ بقائمٍ». ‹ب٦٣›

Contradiction (*tanāquḍ*) is when two propositions differ in affirmation and negation such that the truth of one necessarily entails the falsehood of the other, and vice versa – such as "Zaid is standing" and "Zaid is not standing."

وشرطٌ لتحقّقِ ‹م٤٧› التناقضِ بينَ القضيّتَينِ الخصوصيّتَينِ وحداتٌ ثمانيـةٌ فلا يتحقّقُ بدونِهـا: وحدةُ الموضوعِ، وحدةُ المحمولِ، وحدةُ المـكانِ، وحـدةُ الزمـانِ، وحدةُ القـوّةِ والفعلِ، وحدةُ الشـرطِ، وحدةُ الجزءِ والكلِّ، وحدةُ الإضافةِ.

A condition for realising contradiction between any two given propositions is the presence of eight unities; contradiction is not realised without them:

1. Unity of the subject (*mawḍūʿ*).
2. Unity of the predicate (*maḥmūl*).
3. Unity of the place (*makān*).
4. Unity of the time (*zamān*).
5. Unity of potentiality and actuality (*quwwah wa fiʿl*).
6. Unity of the condition (*sharṭ*).
7. Unity of the whole and part (*juzʾ wa kull*).
8. Unity in the relation (*iḍāfah*).

وقد اجتمعتْ في هذَينِ البيتَينِ:

در تناقض هشت وحدت شرط دان * وحـدت موضوع ومحمـول ومكان

وحـدت شـرط واضافه جـزء وكلّ * قـوّه فعـل اسـت در آخـر زمـان (د۱۱۸)

These eight unities are summed up in the following verse:

Know the conditions of contradiction are eight unities: *
    unity of subject, predicate, place,
Unity of condition, relation, part and whole, *
    potentiality and actuality, and – lastly – time.

فإذا اختلفتا فيها لم تتناقضا، نحوُ:

Hence, when two [propositions] differ in the unities, they do not contradict each other, as in:

١. «زيدٌ قائمٌ، وعمرٌو ليسَ بقائمٍ».

٢. «وزيدٌ قاعدٌ، وزيدٌ ليسَ بقائمٍ».

٣. «وزيـدٌ موجـودٌ» أي: في الـدارِ، و «زيدٌ ليسَ بموجـودٍ» أي: في السوقِ.

٤ . و «زيدٌ نائمٌ» أي: في الليلِ، و «زيدٌ ليسَ بنائمٍ» أي: في النهارِ.

٥ . و «زيـدٌ متحـرّكُ الأصابعِ» أي: بشـرطِ كونِه كاتبًا، و «زيدٌ ليسَ (م٤٨) بكاتبٍ» أي: بشرطِ كونِه غيرَ كاتبٍ.

1. "Zaid is standing," and "'Amr is not standing."
2. "Zaid is sitting," and "Zaid is not standing."
3. "Zaid is present," i.e. at home, and "Zaid is not present," i.e. in the market.
4. "Zaid is asleep," i.e. at night, and "Zaid is not asleep," i.e. during the day.
5. "Zaid is moving his fingers," i.e. under the condition of him writing, and "Zaid is not moving his fingers," i.e. under the condition of him not writing.

٦ . و «الخمرُ في الدَّنِّ مسـكرٌ» أي: بالقوّةِ، و «الخمرُ ليسَ بمسـكرٍ في الدنِّ» أي: بالفعلِ.

٧ . و «الزنجيُّ أسودُ» أي: كلُّه، و «الزنجيُّ ليسَ بأسودَ» أي: جزئُه، أعني: أسنانُه.

٨ . و «زيدٌ أبٌ» أي: لبكرٍ، و «زيدٌ ليسَ بأبٍ» أي: لخالدٍ.

6. "Wine in the decanter is intoxicating," i.e. potentially, and "Wine in the decanter is not intoxicating," i.e. actually.
7. "The black person is black," i.e. entirely, and "The black person is not black," i.e. referring to a part, i.e. his teeth.
8. "Zaid is a father," i.e. to Bakr, and "Zaid is not a father," i.e. to Khālid.

وبعضُهــم اكتفــوا بوحدتَيــنِ، أي: وحــدةِ الموضــوعِ والمحمــولِ، لاندماجِ البواقي فيهما.

Some scholars[43] held that only two unities – unity of the subject and unity of the predicate – are sufficient, since the other unities are encompassed within them.

---

43   e.g. al-Fārābī. Cf. Dār al-Malik edition, 119.

وبعضُهم قنعوا (ب٦٤) بوحدةِ النسبةِ؛ لأنَّ وحدَها مستلزمةٌ بجميعِ الوحداتِ. (د١١٩)

Others[44] were content with a unity of relation, since it alone implies all the other unities.

فصلٌ [تناقضُ القضايا المسورةِ والموجّهةِ]

CONTRADICTION OF BOUNDED AND
MODAL PROPOSITIONS

لا بـدَّ فـي التناقضِ في المحصورتَينِ مِن كونِ القضيّتَينِ مختلفتَينِ في الكمِّ، أعني: الكلّيّةِ والجزئيّةِ.

For contradiction to occur between two bounded propositions, it is necessary that the two propositions differ in quantity (*kamm*), meaning one must be universal and the other particular.

فإذا كانتْ إحداهما كلّيّةً كانتْ الأخرىٰ جزئيّةً؛ لأنَّ الكلّيّتانِ قد تَكذِبانِ، كما تقولُ: «كلُّ حيوانٍ إنسانٌ»، و«لا شيءَ مِن الحيوانِ بإنسانٍ».

If one proposition is universal, the other must be particular, because two universals can both be false – as in "Every animal is a human" and "No animal is a human."

والجزئيّتَينِ قـد تَصدُقانِ، كقولِكَ: «بعـضُ الحيوانِ إنسانٌ»، و«بعـضُ الحيـوانِ ليـسَ بإنسانٍ». ويكونُ ذلكَ في كلِّ مـادّةٍ يكونُ الموضوعُ أعمَّ فيها.

Two particular propositions can both be true – as in "Some animals are human" and "Some animals are not human." This occurs in every matter where the subject is more general.

---

44   e.g. the commentator of *Al-Maṭāliʿ*. Cf. Dār al-Malik edition, 119.

ولا بـدَّ في تناقضِ القضايـا الموجَّهةِ مِن الاخـتلافِ في الجهةِ،

فنقيـضُ الضروريّةِ المطلقةِ الممكنةُ العامّةُ، ونقيـضُ الدائمةِ المطلقةِ

المطلقةُ العامّةُ، (م٤٩، ب٦٥) ونقيـضُ المشـروطةِ العامّةِ الحينيّـةُ

الممكنـةُ، ونقيـضُ العرفيّةِ العامّةِ الحينيّةُ المطلقةُ، وهذا في البسـائطِ

الموجَّهةِ. (د١٢٠)

For contradiction to occur in modal propositions, there must
be a difference in the mode (*jihah*). Thus:

- The contradictory of the absolute necessary (*ḍarūriyyah
  muṭlaqah*) is the general possible (*mumkinah ʿāmmah*).
- The contradictory of the absolute perpetual (*dāʾimah muṭlaqah*)
  is the general absolute (*muṭlaqah ʿāmmah*).
- The contradictory of the general conditional (*mashrūṭah ʿāmmah*) is the possible occasional (*ḥīniyyah mumkinah*).[45]
- The contradictory of the general customary (*ʿurfiyyah ʿāmmah*)
  is the absolute occasional (*ḥīniyyah muṭlaqah*).[46]

This applies to simple modal propositions.

ونقائـضُ المركّبـاتِ مِنهـا مفهـومٌ متردّدٌ بيـنَ نقيضَي بسـائطِها،

والتفصيلُ يُطلبُ مِن مطوّلاتِ الفنِّ. (م٥٠)

As for the contradictories of compound modal propositions,
their meaning (*mafhūm*) wavers between the two contradictories
of their simple forms. Further details are sought in the extensive
works of the discipline.

---

45 The *possible occasional* is a proposition in which it is asserted to remove
    necessity as befits the description of the opposing side. Such as your statement:
    "All who have pneumonia is possible that he coughs during some of the times
    while he has pneumonia." Cf. al-Bushrā edition, 66.

46 The *absolute occasional* is a proposition in which it is asserted to affirm or
    negate an action during some of the times it describes the subject. For example:
    "All who have pneumonia coughs, actually, during some of the times he has
    pneumonia." Cf. al-Bushrā edition, 66.

 فصلٌ [تناقضُ الشرطيّاتِ]

ويُشــترطُ في أخذِ نقائضِ الشــرطيّاتِ الاتّفاقُ في الجنسِ والنوعِ، والمخالفةُ في الكيفِ. ‹د١٢١›

فنقيضُ المتّصلةِ اللزوميّةِ الموجبةِ سالبةٌ متّصلةٌ لزوميّةٌ.

ونقيضُ المنفصلةِ العناديّةِ الموجبةِ سالبةٌ منفصلةٌ عناديّةٌ.

وهكذا.

To obtain the contradictories of conditional propositions, agreement between the genus[47] and species and a disparity in the quality[48] are required – so:

The contradictory of an affirmative implicative conjunctive is a negative implicative conjunctive.

The contradictory of an affirmative oppositional disjunctive is a negative oppositional disjunctive.

And so forth.

فإذا قلــتَ: «دائمًــا كلّما كانَ أ ب فـ ج د» ‹ب٦٦› كانَ نقيضُه «ليسَ كلّما كانَ أ ب فـ ج د».

وإذا قلتَ: «دائمًا إمّا أنْ يكونَ هذا العددُ زوجًا أو فردًا»، فنقيضُه «ليسَ دائمًا إمّا أنْ يكونَ هذا العددُ زوجًا أو فردًا».

Hence, if you say "Always, whenever A is B, then C is D," its contradictory is "Not always, whenever A is B, then C is D."

And if you say "Always, either this number is even or odd," its contradictory is "Not always, either this number is even or odd."

---

47   Genus: Conjunctive and disjunctive; species: implication, opposition, and agreement. Cf. Dār al-Malik edition, 121.

48   (Tr:) Here, *genus* refers to conjunctive or disjunctive; *species* to necessity, antagonistic, harmonious; and *quality* to affirmative, negative.

فصلٌ [في العكسِ المستوي]

«العكسُ المستوي»، ويُقالُ له: «العكسُ المستقيمُ» أيضًا، وهو: عبارةٌ عـن جعلِ الجزءِ الأوّلِ ‹د١٢٢› مِن القضيّةِ ثانيًا، والجزءِ الثاني أوّلًا، مع بقاءِ الصدقِ والكيفِ.

Equivalent conversion (ʿaks mustawī), also called *straight conversion* (ʿaks mustaqīm), refers to interchanging the first and second parts of a proposition while preserving its truth and quality.

فالسـالبةُ الكلّيّةُ تنعكسُ كنفسِـها، كقولِكَ: «لا شيءَ مِن الإنسانِ بحجرٍ»، ينعكـسُ إلىٰ قولِكَ: «لا شـيءَ مِن الحجرِ بإنسانٍ»، بدليلِ الخُلفِ، تقريرُه: أنَّه لو لم يصدق «لا شـيءَ مِن الحجرِ بإنسانٍ» عندَ صـدقِ قولِنا: «لا ‹م٥١› شـيءَ مِن الإنسانِ بحجرٍ»، لصدقَ نقيضُه، أعني قولَنا: «بعضُ الحجرِ إنسانٌ»، فنضمُّه مع الأصلِ ونقولُ: «بعضُ الحجرِ إنسانٌ ولا شيءَ مِن الإنسانِ بحجرٍ»، ينتجُ: «بعضُ الحجرِ ليسَ بحجرٍ»، فيلزمُ سلبُ الشيءِ عن نفسِه، وذلكَ محالٌ. ‹ب٦٧، د١٢٣›

The universal negative proposition converts like itself. As in your statement "No human is a stone," which converts to "No stone is a human." This follows from proof of absurdity (*dalīl al-khulf*),[49] which is formulated as follows: if it were not true that "No stone is a human" when our statement: "No human is a stone" is true, then its contradictory would be true, that is, our statement: "Some stone is a human." If we join this with the original statement: "Some stone is a human; no human is a stone; thus some stones are not stones." This results in self-negation, which is impossible.

---

49   Which refers to affirming the sought conclusion by invalidating its contradictory. Cf. Dār al-Malik, 123. See page 107.

والسـالبةُ الجزئيّةُ لا تنعكـسُ لزومًـا؛ لجـوازِ عمـومِ الموضـوعِ في الحمليّـةِ، والمقـدَّمِ في الشـرطيّةِ، مثلًا يصدقُ ‹‹بعـضُ الحيوانِ ليسَ بإنسانٍ››، وليسَ يصدقُ ‹‹بعضُ الإنسانِ ليسَ بحيوانٍ››.

The particular negative does not necessarily convert, due to the possibility of the subject's generality in the predicating proposition and of the antecedent's generality in the conditional proposition – for example: "Some animals are not humans" is true, while "Some humans are not animals" is not true.

والموجبةُ الكليّـةُ تنعكسُ إلىٰ موجبةٍ جزئيّةٍ، كقولِنا: ‹‹كلُّ إنسانٍ حيـوانٌ››، ينعكـسُ إلـىٰ قولِنا: ‹‹بعـضُ الحيوانِ إنسـانٌ››، ولا ينعكسُ إلىٰ موجبةٍ كليّةٍ؛ لأنَّه يجوزُ أنْ يكونَ المحمولُ والتالي عامًّا كما في مثالِنا، فلا يصدقُ ‹‹كلُّ حيوانٍ إنسانٌ››.

The universal affirmative proposition converts to a particular affirmative – for example, "Every human is an animal" converts to "Some animals are humans." It does not convert to a universal affirmative, since the predicate and consequent may be general, as in our example: "Every animal is a human" is not true.

وهاهنا شكٌّ تقريرُه: أنَّ قولَنا: ‹‹كلُّ شيخٍ كانَ شابًا››، موجبةٌ كليّةٌ صادقةٌ مع أنَّ عكسَه: ‹‹بعضُ الشباب كانَ شيخًا›› ليسَ بصادقٍ؟.

وأُجيبَ عنه: بأنَّ عكسَه ليسَ ما ذكرتَ، بل عكسُه: ‹‹بعضُ مَن كانَ شابًا شيخٌ››. (د ١٢٤)

وقد يجابُ بوجهٍ (م ٥٢) آخرَ وهو: أن (ب ٦٨) حفظَ النسبةِ ليسَ بضروريٍّ في العكسِ، فعكسُه ‹‹بعضُ الشبابِ يكونُ شيخًا››، وهو صادقٌ لا محالةَ.

Here arises a cause for doubt (*ishkāl*): our statement "Every elder was a youth" is a true universal affirmative, yet its apparent converse "Some of the youth were elders" is not true.

The answer is that the correct converse is not as stated but rather "Some of those who were young are elders." Another possible answer is that preserving the relation is not necessary in conversion, so its converse is "Some youth are elders" – which is true without a doubt.

والموجبــةُ الجزئيّــةُ تنعكـسُ إلـىٰ موجبــةٍ جزئيّــةٍ، كقولِنــا: «بعضُ الحيوانِ إنسانٌ»، ينعكسُ إلىٰ قولِنا: «بعضُ الإنسانِ حيوانٌ».

A particular affirmative converts to a particular affirmative – such as "Some animals are humans" converts to "Some humans are animals."

وقــد يــوردُ علـىٰ انعكاسِ الموجبــةِ الجزئيّةِ كنفسِــها إيــرادٌ وهو أنَّ «بعــضَ الوتدِ في الحائطِ» صادقٌ، وعكسُــه، أعنـي: «بعضُ الحائطِ في الوتدِ»، ليسَ بصادقٍ؟

والجواب: أنّا لا نسلِّمُ أنَّ عكسَ هذهِ القضيّةِ ما قلتَ مِن «بعضِ الحائطِ في الوتدِ»، بل عكسُه: «بعضُ ما في الحائطِ وتدٌ»، ولا مُريةَ في صدقِه. (د١٢٥)

An objection might be raised against the conversion of the particular affirmative: "Some of the pegs are in the wall" is true, yet its apparent converse "Some of the wall is in the pegs" is not. The response is that this is not the correct converse – rather, the correct converse is "Some of what is in the wall is a peg," and there is no doubt about its truth.

وباقي مسائلِ العكوسِ مِن عكسِ الموجَّهاتِ والشرطيّاتِ فمذكورٌ في المطوَّلاتِ. (ب٦٩)

The remaining issues related to the conversion of modal and conditional propositions are discussed in more detail in extensive works.

CONTRADICTORY CONVERSION   فصلٌ [في عكسِ النقيضِ]

«عكسُ النقيضِ»، هو: جعلُ نقيضِ الجزءِ الأوّلِ مِن القضيّةِ ثانيًا، ونقيضِ الجزءِ الثاني أوّلًا، مع بقاءِ الصدقِ والكيفِ. هذا أسلوبُ المتقدّمينَ. (د١٢٦)

Contradictory conversion (‘aks al-naqīḍ, lit. conversion of the contradictory) is the process of moving the negation of the first part of a proposition to the second part and the negation of the second part to the first part, while preserving truth and quality. This was the method employed by the early logicians.

فتنعكسُ الموجبةُ الكلّيّةُ بهـذا العكسِ كنفسِـها، كقولِنا: «كلُّ إنسانٍ حيوانٌ» ينعكسُ إلىٰ قولِنا: «كلُّ لا حيوانٍ لا إنسانٌ».

Thus, a universal affirmative converts into itself in this type of conversion – such as "Every human is an animal" converts to "Every non-animal is a non-human."

والموجبةُ الجزئيّةُ لا تنعكسُ هـذا العكـسَ؛ لأنَّ قولَنـا: «بعضُ الحيوانِ لاإنسانٌ» صادقٌ، وعكسُه، أعني: «بعضُ الإنسانِ لاحيوانٌ»، كاذبٌ.

A particular affirmative does not convert in this manner, since "Some animals are non-humans" is true, but its converse "Some humans are non-animals" is false.

والسـالبةُ الكلّيّةُ تنعكسُ إلىٰ سالبةٍ جزئيّةٍ، (م٥٣) تقولُ: «لا شيءَ مِن الإنسانِ بفرسٍ»، وتقولُ في عكسِه بهذا العكسِ: «بعضُ اللافرسِ

ليسَ بلاإنسانٍ» إلىٰ جزئيّةٍ، ولا تقولُ: «لا شيءَ مِن اللافرسِ بلاإنسانٍ»؛ لصدقِ نقيضِه، أعني: «بعضُ اللافرسِ لاإنسانٌ» كالجدارِ.

A universal negative converts to a particular negative in this manner – "No human is a horse" converts to "Some non-horses are not non-humans." It does not convert to "No non-horse is a non-human," since its contradictory is true, namely "Some non-horses are non-humans," such as walls.

والسـالبةُ الجزئيّةُ تنعكسُ إلىٰ: سـالبةٍ جزئيّةٍ، كقولِكَ: «بعضُ الحيـوانِ ليسَ بإنسـانٍ»، تنعكسُ إلىٰ قولِكَ: «بعضُ اللاإنسـانِ ليسَ بلاحيوانٍ» كالفرسِ (ب ٧٠).

A particular negative converts to a particular negative – for example, "Some animals are not human" converts to "Some non-humans are not non-animals," such as horses.

* * *

وعكوسُ الموجّهاتِ والشرطياتِ(٥٠) مذكورةٌ في الكتبِ الطوالِ. وهاهنا قد تمّتْ مباحثُ القضايا وأحكامِها. (د ١٢٧)

The conversion of modal and conditional propositions is discussed in extensive works.[51]

---

50   al-Bushrā edition has (الشرطيات); it is missing in al-Madīnah edition.

51   The two perpetuals and generals convert as absolute occasionals. For example: whenever "Necessarily or always every human is an animal" is true, "The animal is a human in fact when it is an animal," is true. And when "Necessarily or always every writer moves fingers so long as he is a writer" is true, "Some who move fingers are writers in fact."

    And two particulars convert as absolute occasionals, not always. Two temporals, two existentials, and the general absolute convert as absolute, i.e. each one of those five propositions converts into a general absolute.

    There is no conversion for negative possibles.

    Perpetuals always convert as absolute perpetuals.

    Two generals convert as general conventionals.

With this, we have concluded the topics on propositions and their rules in logic.

Two specials convert as conventional non-perpetuals in some.
The rest do not convert.
Cf. al-Bushrā edition, 69; al-Madīnah edition, 54; Dār al-Malik edition, 127.

4

ARGUMENTS AND SYLLOGISMS

فصلٌ [مقدّمةُ مباحثِ الحججِ]

وإذْ قد فرغنا مِن مباحثِ القضايا والعكوسِ التي كانتْ مِن مبادئِ الحجّةِ، فحريٌّ بنا أنْ نتكلّمَ في مباحثِ الحجّةِ، فنقولُ:

Having completed our discussions on propositions and conversions, which are fundamental principles of argumentation (*ḥujjah*), it is now fitting for us to discuss the study of arguments. So, we say:

الحجّـةُ علـى ثلاثةِ أقسامٍ: أحدُها: القياسُ، وثانيها: الاستقراءُ، وثالثُها: التمثيلُ. فلنبيّنْ هذهِ الثلاثةَ في ثلاثةِ فصول. ‹م٥٤›

Arguments fall into three categories.
The first is syllogism (*qiyās*).
The second is induction (*istiqrā'*).
The third is analogy (*tamthīl*).
We will clarify these three topics in three separate sections.

فصلٌ: في القياسِ

وهـو: قولٌ مؤلَّفٌ ‹ب٧١›، مِن قضايا، ‹د١٢٨›، يلزمُ عنها قولٌ آخرُ بعدَ تسليمِ تلكَ القضايا.

A *syllogism* (*qiyās*) is a statement composed of propositions that logically entail another statement upon conceding those propositions.

فإنْ كانتِ النتيجةُ أو نقيضُها مذكورًا فيه يُسمّىٰ: «استثنائيًّا»، كقولِنا: «إنْ كانَ زيدٌ إنسانًا كانَ حيوانًا، لكنَّه إنسانٌ»، ينتجُ: «فهو حيوانٌ». و«إنْ كانَ زيدٌ حمارًا كانَ ناهقًا، لكنَّه ليسَ بناهقٍ»، ينتجُ: «إنَّه ليسَ بحمارٍ».

If the conclusion or its contradictory is explicitly stated, it is called *excepting* (*istithnā'ī*) – as in "If Zaid is a human, he is an animal; but he is a human; thus he is an animal"; and "If Zaid is a donkey, he is braying; but he is not braying; thus he is not a donkey."

وإنْ لم تكنِ النتيجةُ ونقيضُها مذكورًا يُسمّىٰ: «اقترانيًّا»، كقولِكَ: «زيدٌ إنسانٌ، وكلُّ إنسانٍ حيوانٌ»، ينتجُ: «زيدٌ حيوانٌ». ﴿د١٢٩﴾

If neither the conclusion or its contradictory is explicitly stated, it is called *connecting* (*iqtirānī*) – as in "Zaid is a human; every human is an animal; thus Zaid is an animal."

فصلٌ: في القياسِ الاقترانيِّ

CONNECTING SYLLOGISM

وهو قسمانِ: حمليٌّ، وشرطيٌّ.

A connecting syllogism (*qiyās iqtirānī*) has two types: *predicating* (*ḥamlī*) and *conditional* (*sharṭī*).

وموضوعُ النتيجةِ في القياسِ ﴿ب٧٢﴾ يُسمّىٰ: «أصغرَ»؛ لكونِه أقلَّ أفرادٍ في الأغلبِ.

ومحمولُه يُسمّىٰ: «أكبرَ»؛ لكونِه أكثرَ أفرادٍ غالبًا.

The subject of the result in the syllogism is called the *minor term* (*aṣghar*) because it usually has fewer instances.

Its predicate is called the *major term* (*akbar*) because it generally has more instances.

والقضيّةُ التي جُعلت جزءَ قياسٍ تُسمّىٰ: «مقدّمةً».

والمقدّمةُ التي فيها الأصغرُ تُسمّىٰ: «صغرىٰ».

والتي فيها الأكبرُ: «كبرىٰ».

والجزءُ الذي تكرّرَ بينَهما يُسمّىٰ: «حدًّا أوسطَ».

The proposition that forms a part of the syllogism is called a *premise* (muqaddimah).

The premise containing the minor term is called the *minor premise* (ṣughrā).

The premise containing the major term is called the *major premise* (kubrā).

The term that appears in both premises is called the *middle term* (ḥadd awsaṭ).

واقترانُ الصغرىٰ بالوسطىٰ يُسمّىٰ: «قرينةً» و «ضربًا».

والهيئةُ الحاصلةُ مِن كيفيّةِ وضعِ الأوسطِ عندَ الأصغرِ والأكبرِ تُسمّىٰ: «شكلًا». (د ١٣٠)

The linking of the minor premise with the middle term is called a *connection* (qarīnah) and *mood* (ḍarb).

The configuration resulting from the placement of the middle term between the minor and major terms is called a *figure* (shakl).

والأشكالُ أربعةٌ. وجهُ الضبطِ أنْ يُقالَ: الحدُّ الأوسطُ:

There are four figures. They are determined by the placement of the middle term, as follows:

إمّا محمولُ الصغرىٰ وموضوعُ الكبرىٰ، كما في قولِنا: «العالَمُ متغيّرٌ، وكلُّ متغيّرٍ حادثٌ»، ينتجُ: «العالَمُ حادثٌ»، فهو الشكلُ الأوّلُ.

1. If the middle term is the predicate of the minor premise and the subject of the major premise, it is the first figure (al-shakl al-awwal) – such as "The world is changing; everything changing is originated; thus the world is originated." This is the *first figure* (*al-shakl al-awwal*).

وإنْ كان محمـولًا فيهمـا فهـو الشـكلُ الثاني، كما تقولُ: «كلُّ إنسانٍ حيوانٌ، ولا شيءَ مِن الحجرِ بحيوانٍ»، فالنتيجةُ: «لا شيءَ مِن الإنسانِ بحجرٍ».

2. If the middle term is the predicate in both premises, it is the *second figure* (*shakl thānī*) – such as "Every human is an animal; no stone is an animal; thus no human is a stone."

وإنْ كان موضوعًا فيهما فهو الشـكلُ الثالثُ، نحوُ: «كلُّ إنسانٍ حيوانٌ، وبعضُ الإنسـانِ (م٥٦) كاتبٌ»، ينتـجُ: «بعـضُ الحيـوانِ كاتبٌ». (ب٧٣، د١٣١٥)

3. If the middle term is the subject in both premises, it is the *third figure* (*shakl thālith*) – such as "Every human is an animal; some humans are writers; thus some animals are writers."

وإنْ كان موضوعًا فـي الصغرىٰ ومحمولًا في الكبرىٰ فهو الشـكلُ الرابعُ، نحوُ قولِنا: «كلُّ إنسانٍ حيوانٌ، وبعضُ الكاتبِ إنسانٌ»، ينتجُ: «بعضُ الحيوانِ كاتبٌ».

4. If the middle term is the subject in the minor premise and the predicate in the major premise, it is the *fourth figure* (*shakl rābiʿ*) – such as "Every human is an animal; some writers are humans; thus some animals are writers."[52]

---

52 (Tr:) A summary of the four figures, combining the given examples and employing the abbreviations mentioned earlier and used in

    First: [J is B]. All [B is D]. So [J is D].
    Second: All [J is B]. No [A is B]. So no [J is A].
    Third: Every [B is J]. Some [B is A]. So some [J is A].

FIRST FIGURE

فصلٌ [الشكلُ الأوّلُ]

وأشــرفُ الأشــكالِ مِن الأربعةِ الشــكلُ الأوّلُ. ولذلكَ كانَ إنتاجُه بيّنًا بديهيًّا يسـبقُ الذهنُ فيه إلى النتيجةِ سـبقًا طبيعيًّا مِن دونِ حاجةٍ إلىٰ فكرٍ وتأمّلٍ.

The noblest of the four forms is the first figure. This is why its conclusion is clear and self-evident, and the mind races to the conclusion naturally, without any need for thought or contemplation.

وله شرائطُ وضروبٌ.

It has conditions and moods.

أمّا الشــرائطُ فاثنـانِ. أحدُهما: إيجابُ الصغـرىٰ، وثانيهما: كلّيّةُ الكبرىٰ.

فإنْ يُفقدا ‹د١٣٢› معًا أو يُفقد أحدُهما لا تلزمُ النتيجةُ، كما يظهرُ عندَ التأمّلِ.

The conditions are two: the minor premise must be affirmative, and the major premise must be universal.

If both or one of them is missing, the conclusion does not follow, as is apparent upon reflection.

وأمّا الضروبُ فأربعةٌ؛ لأنَّ الاحتمالاتِ ‹م٥٦› في كلِّ شـكلٍ سـتّةَ عشـرَ؛ لأنَّ الصغـرىٰ أربعـةٌ، والكبـرىٰ أيضًـا أربعةٌ - أعنـي: الموجبةَ الكلّيّـةَ، والموجبـةَ الجزئيّةَ، والسـالبةَ الكلّيّةَ، والجزئيّةَ - والأربعةُ في الأربعةِ ستّةَ عشرَ.

Fourth: Every [B is J]. Some [A is J]. So some [J are A].
The quantifiers are not relevant here; they are relevant in each form's mood.

There are four moods since there are sixteen possibilities for each figure. This is because there are four minor premises and four major premises (i.e. the universal affirmative, particular affirmative, universal negative, and particular negative). Four times four is sixteen.

وأسقطتْ شـرائطُ الشكلِ الأوّلِ اثنا عشرَ، وهي: الصغرى السالبةُ الكلّيّةُ مع الكبرياتِ الأربعِ، والصغرى السالبةُ الجزئيّةُ مع تلكَ ‹ب٧٤› الأربعِ. وهذهِ ثمانية.

والكبـرى الموجبـةُ الجزئيّةُ والسـالبةُ الجزئيّةُ مع الصغـرى الموجبةِ الجزئيّةِ والكلّيّةِ وهذهِ أربعةٌ.

The conditions on the first figure eliminate twelve possibilities: the minor premise being a universal negative with each of the four major premises (1–4); the minor premise being a particular negative with each of the four major premises (5–8); and the major premise being a particular affirmative or particular negative with the minor premise being either a particular affirmative or universal affirmative (9–12).

These are four[, making a total of twelve].

فبقي أربعةُ ضروبٍ منتجةٍ. [وهي:]

Thus, four productive moods remain. [See Figure 1 on page 92 for an explanation of how modes are elimited and remain.]

الضربُ الأوّلُ: مركّبٌ مِن موجبةٍ كلّيّةٍ صغرىٰ وموجبةٍ كلّيّةٍ كبرىٰ، ينتـجُ: موجبـةً كلّيّةً، ‹د١٣٣› نحوَ: «كلُّ ج ب وكلّ ب د»، ينتجُ: «كلُّ ج د».

The first mood consists of a universal affirmative minor premise and a universal affirmative major premise, producing a universal affirmative conclusion – for example, "Every J is B; all B is D; thus all J is D."

FIGURE 1. Productive and Non-Productive Modes for Form I

		MAJOR PREMISE			
		UNIVERSAL AFFIRMATIVE	PARTICULAR AFFIRMATIVE	UNIVERSAL NEGATIVE	PARTICULAR NEGATIVE
	UNIVERSAL AFFIRMATIVE	Universal Affirmative (Mode 1)	9 ☠	Negative Universal (Mode 2)	10 ☠
MINOR PREMISE	PARTICULAR AFFIRMATIVE	Universal Affirmative (Mode 3)	11 ☠	Negative Particular (Mode 4)	12 ☠
	UNIVERSAL NEGATIVE	1 ☠	2 ☠	3 ☠	4 ☠
	PARTICULAR NEGATIVE	5 ☠	6 ☠	7 ☠	8 ☠

This table shows how the conditions for Form I result in four productive modes, along with what those modes product.

The condition for Form I are that minor premise must be affirmative, and the major premise must be universal. When examined in detail...

- The minor premise being a universal negative with the four major premises eliminates 1–4 ☠ on the table.
- The minor premise being negative particular with the four major premise eliminates 5–8 ☠.
- The major premise being a particular affirmative or particular negative with the minor premise being a particular affirmative or universal affirmative eliminates 9–12 ☠.

Four productive modes remain:

1. "All J are B, all B are A, so all J are A."
2. "All J are B, no B are A, so no J are A."
3. "Some J are B, all B are A, so some J are A."
4. "Some J are B, no B are A, so some J are not A."

والضربُ الثاني: مؤلَّفٌ مِن موجبةٍ كلّيّةٍ صغرىٰ وسالبةٍ كلّيّةٍ كبرىٰ، ينتجُ: سـالبةً كلّيّةً، نحوَ: «كلُّ إنسـانٍ حيوانٌ، ولا شـيءَ مِن الحيوانِ بحجرٍ»، ينتجُ: «لا شيءَ مِن الإنسانِ بحجرٍ».

The second mood consists of a universal affirmative minor premise and a universal negative major premise, producing a universal negative conclusion – for example, "All humans are animals; no animal is a stone; thus no human is a stone."

والضربُ الثالـثُ: ملتئمٌ مِـن موجبةٍ جزئيّةٍ صغرىٰ، وموجبةٍ كلّيّةٍ كبرىٰ، والنتيجةُ موجبةٌ جزئيّةٌ، نحوُ: «بعضُ الحيوانِ فرسٌ، وكلُّ فرسٍ صهّالٌ»، ينتجُ: «بعضُ الحيوانِ صهال».

The third mood consists of a particular affirmative minor premise and a universal affirmative major premise, producing a particular affirmative conclusion – for example, "Some animals are horses; all horses are neighing; thus some animals are neighing."

والضربُ الرابعُ: مزدوجٌ مِن موجبةٍ جزئيّةٍ صغرىٰ، (ب٧٥) وسالبةٍ كلّيّةٍ كبرىٰ، ينتجُ: سالبةً جزئيّةً، كقولِنا: «بعضُ الحيوانِ ناطقٌ، ولا شيءَ مِن الناطقِ بناهقٍ»، فالنتيجةُ: «بعضُ الحيوانِ ليسَ بناهقٍ».

The fourth mood consists of a particular affirmative minor premise and a universal negative major premise, producing a particular negative conclusion – for example, "Some animals are rational beings; no rational being is braying; thus some animals are not braying."

تنبيهٌ: إنتاجُ الموجبةِ الكلّيّـةِ مِن خواصِّ الشـكلِ الأوّلِ، كما أنَّ الإنتاجَ للنتائجِ الأربعةِ أيضًا مِن خصائصِه.

والصغرى الممكنةُ غيرُ منتجةٍ في هذا الشكلِ. (د١٣٤)

Warning. Producing a universal affirmative conclusion is a characteristic of the first figure, just as producing all the four types of conclusions is also among its characteristics.

The possible minor premise does not produce a valid conclusion in this figure.[53]

فقــد وضــحَ بما ذكرنـا أنَّه لا بدَّ^(٥٤) في هذا الشكلِ كيفًا إيجابُ الصغرىٰ، وكمًّا كلّيّةُ الكبرىٰ، وجهةً فعليّةُ الصغرىٰ. (م٥٧)

Thus, as mentioned, this figure requires an affirmative quality for the minor premise, a universal scope for the major premise, and an actualised direction for the minor premise.[55]

SECOND FIGURE   فصلٌ [شروطُ إنتاجِ الشكلِ الثاني]

ويُشــترطُ في إنتاجِ الشــكلِ الثاني بحسبِ الكيفِ، أي: الإيجابِ والسـلبِ، اخــتلافُ المقدّمتَيـنِ، فإنْ كانتْ الصغرىٰ موجبةً كانتْ الكبـرىٰ سـالبةً وبالعكـسِ، (ب٧٦) وبحسـبِ الكـمِّ، أي: الكلّيّـةِ والجزئيّـةِ، كلّيّةُ الكبرىٰ، وإلَّا يلـزمُ الاختلافُ الموجِبُ لعدمِ الإنتاجِ، أي: صدقِ القياسِ مع إيجابِ النتيجةِ تارةً، ومع سلبِها أخرىٰ.

The second figure has two conditions for productivity. As regards quality (i.e. affirmation or negation), the two premises must differ – if the minor premise is affirmative, the major must be negative, and vice versa.

As regards quantity (i.e. universal or particular), the major premise must be universal; otherwise the same syllogism would

---

53   See simple and complex modal propositions, starting on pages 58 and 61.

54   al-Madīnah edition has (بّ) and not (بـ لا).

55   Quality refers to affirmative or negative.
      Scope refers to universal or particular.
      Direction refers to potential or actual. Cf. al-Madīnah edition, 57.

produce an affirmative conclusion at times and a negative one at others, resulting in inconsistency and a lack of productivity.

ونتيجةُ هذا الشكلِ لا تكونُ إلّا سالبةً. (د١٣٥)

The conclusion of this figure is always negative.

وضروبُه الناتجةُ أربعةٌ:

It has four productive moods.

أحدُها: مِن كلّيّتَينِ والصغرىٰ موجبةٌ، ينتجُ: سالبةً كلّيّةً، كقولِنا: «كلُّ ج ب، ولا شيءَ مِن أ ب، فلا شيءَ مِن ج أ».

والدليلُ علىٰ هذا الإنتاجِ: عكسُ الكبرىٰ؛ فإنَّك إذا (م٥٨) عكستَ الكبرىٰ صارتْ: «لا شيءَ مِن ب أ»، وبانضمامِها إلى الصغرىٰ انتظمَ الشكلُ الأوّلُ، وينتجُ النتيجةَ المطلوبةَ. (ب٧٧)

The first consists of two universals where the minor premise is affirmative, producing a universal negative – for example, "Every J is B; no A is B; thus no J is A."

This productivity is demonstrated by the conversion of the major premise: when converted it becomes "No B is A," and when joined with the minor premise the syllogism takes the form of the first figure, yielding the desired conclusion (*matlūb*).

الضربُ الثاني: مِن موجبةٍ كلّيّةٍ كبرىٰ، وسالبةٍ كلّيّةٍ صغرىٰ، كقولِنا: «لا شيءَ مِن ج ب، وكلُّ أ ب»، ينتجُ: «لا شيءَ مِن ج أ».

والدليلُ على الإنتاجِ: عكسُ الصغرىٰ، وجعلُها كبرىٰ، (د١٣٦) ثمَّ عكسُ النتيجةِ.

The second mood consists of a universal affirmative major premise and a universal negative minor premise – for example, "No J is B; every A is B; thus no J is A."

Its productivity is demonstrated by converting the minor premise and making it the major premise, then converting the conclusion.[56]

الضربُ الثالثُ: مِن موجبةٍ جزئيّةٍ صغرىٰ، وسالبةٍ كلّيّةٍ كبرىٰ، ينتجُ سالبةً جزئيّةً، كقولِكَ: «بعضُ ج ب، ولا شيءَ مِن أ ب، فليسَ بعضُ ج أ».

The third mood consists of a particular affirmative minor premise and a universal negative major premise, producing a particular negative conclusion – for example, "Some J is B; no A is B; thus some J is not A."

الضربُ الرابعُ: مِن سالبةٍ جزئيّةٍ صغرىٰ، وموجبةٍ كلّيّةٍ كبرىٰ، ينتجُ سالبةً جزئيّةً، تقولُ: «بعضُ ج ليسَ ب، وكلُّ أ ب، فبعضُ ج ليسَ أ».

The fourth mood consists of a particular negative minor premise and a universal affirmative major premise, producing a particular negative conclusion – for example, "Some J is not B; every A is B; thus some J is not A."

THIRD FIGURE فصلٌ [شروطُ إنتاج الشكلِ الثالثِ]

شــرطُ إنتــاج الشــكلِ الثالثِ: كونُ الصغرىٰ موجبةً، وكونُ إحدى المقدَّمتينِ كلّيّةً.

---

56   (Tr:) The proof proceeds in two steps. First, convert the minor premise ("No J is B" becomes "No B is J") and treat it as the major premise. Paired with the original major premise ("Every A is B") now serving as the minor, the syllogism takes the form of the first figure and yields "No A is J." Second, convert this conclusion to obtain the desired result: "No J is A." This reduction technique, whereby a figure is validated by converting one or more of its premises and reducing it to the first figure.

The conditions for the third figure's productivity are that the minor premise must be affirmative and that one of the premises must be universal.

فضروبُه الناتجةُ ستّةٌ. (د١٣٧)

أحدُها: «كلُّ ب ج، وكلُّ مِنْ[57] ب أ، فبعضُ ج أ».

وثانيها: «كلُّ ب ج، ولا (م٥٩) شيءَ مِن ب أ، فبعضُ ج ليسَ أ».

وثالثُها: «بعضُ ب ج، وكلُّ ب أ، فبعضُ ج أ».

ورابعُها: «بعضُ ب ج، ولا شيءَ مِن ب أ، فبعضُ ج ليسَ أ». (ب٧٨)

وخامسُها: «كلُّ ب ج، وبعضُ ب أ، فبعضُ ج أ».

وسادسُها: «كلُّ ب ج، وبعضُ ب ليسَ أ، فبعضُ ج ليسَ أ».

(د١٣٨)

Its productive moods are six.
The first mood: "Every B is J; every B is A; thus some J is A."
The second mood: "Every B is J; no B is A; thus some J is not A."
The third mood: "Some B is J; every B is A; thus some J is A."
The fourth mood: "Some B is J; no B is A; thus some J is not A."
The fifth mood: "Every B is J; some B is A; thus some J is A."
The sixth mood: "Every B is J; some B is not A; thus some J is not A."

FOURTH FIGURE   فصلٌ [شروطُ انتاجِ الشكلِ الرابعِ]

وشــرائطُ انتاجِ الشــكلِ الرابعِ مع كثرتِها، وقلّة جدواها مذكورةٌ في المبسـوطاتِ، فلا علينا لو تركنا ذكرَها، وكذا شـرائطَ سـائرَ الأشكالِ بحسبِ الجهةِ لا يتحملُ أمثالُ رسالتي هذهِ لبيانِها. (ب٧٩)

───────────

57   al-Bushrā and al-Madīnah editions: (وكلٌّ مِنْ ب أ); another *matn*-only edition: (ولا شيءَ مِن ب أ).

The conditions for the fourth figure's productivity, despite their numerous details and limited utility, are mentioned in the comprehensive works.[58] Thus, omitting them is of no consequence to us.

The same applies to the conditions for other figures based on modality – treatises such as mine do not accommodate their clarification.

فائدةٌ [النتيجةُ في القياسِ تتبعُ أدونَ المقدّمتينِ]

BENEFICIAL POINT: THE RESULT
FOLLOWS THE LOWER PREMISE

ولعلَّكَ علمـتَ مِمّا ألقينا عليـكَ أنَّ النتيجةَ في القياسِ تتبعُ أدونَ المقدّمتينِ في الكيفِ والكمِّ.

والأدونُ في الكيفِ هو: السلبُ، وفي الكمِّ هو: الجزئيّةُ.

Perhaps you have learned from what we have presented that the conclusion in a syllogism follows the lower-ranking premise in both quality and quantity – the lower-ranking attribute for quality being negation, and for quantity being particularity.

فالقياسُ المركّبُ مِن موجبةٍ وسالبةٍ ينتجُ سالبةً.

Thus, when the syllogism consists of one affirmative and one negative, it produces a negative conclusion.

والمركّبُ مِن كلّيّةٍ وجزئيّةٍ إنّما ينتجُ جزئيّةً.

A syllogism consisting of a universal premise and a particular premise only produces a particular conclusion.

أمّا المركّبُ مِن كلّيّتينِ فربّما ينتجُ كلّيّةً، وقد ينتجُ جزئيّةً.

---

58   (Tr:) The conditions for the fourth figure require one of two things: (1) that both premises must be affirmative, and the minor premise also must be universal; or that (2) one premise must be affirmative and one must be negative, and one of them also must be universal.

However, a syllogism consisting of two universal premises may yield either a universal or a particular conclusion.[59]

---

59 Some English books mention eight rules for syllogisms. Some of these rules are redundant, and many of them appear in our own text, though not all together. These rules are:

1. A syllogism must have only three terms: major, middle, and minor.

2. A term cannot be broader in the conclusion than it is in the premises.

3. The middle term must never appear in the conclusion.

4. The middle term must be distributed at least once (n.b. this is not explicitly covered in this book).

5. From two negative premises, no conclusion follows.

6. When both premises are affirmative, the conclusion cannot be negative.

7. The conclusion always follows the lower-ranking premise (i.e., particular and negative).

8. From two particular premises, no conclusion follows.

See Scott M. Sullivan, *An Introduction to Traditional Logic* (Houston: Classical Theist Publishing, 2013), 121–124.

FIGURE 2. Summary of Forms I–IV and their Productive Modes

Form I. The minor premise must be affirmative; the major premise must be universal.

It has four productive forms.

1 "All J are B, all B are A, so all J are A."
2 "All J are B, no B are A, so no J are A."
3 "Some J are B, all B are A, so some J are A."
4 "Some J are B, no B are A, so some J are not A."

Figure II. One premise must be affirmative and one negative; the major premise must be universal.

It also has four productive modes.

1 "All J are B, no A are B, so no J are A."
2 "No J are B, all A are B, so no J are A."
3 "Some J are B, no A are B, so some J are not A."
4 "Some J are not B, all A are B, so some J are not A."

Figure III. The major premise must be affirmative; one premise must be universal.

It has six productive modes.

1 "All B are J, all B are A, so some J are A."
2 "All B are J, no B are A, so some J are not A.
3 "Some B are J, all B are A, so some J are A."
4 "Some B are J, no B are A, so some J are not A."
5 "All B are J, some B are A, so some J are A."
6 "All B are J, some B are not A, some J are not A."

Figure IV. Either both of the premises are affirmative and the minor premise is universal; or one is affirmative and the other negative, and one premise is universal.

It has eight productive modes.

1 "All B are J, all A are B, so some J are A."
2 All B are J, some A are B, so some J are A."
3 "No B are J, all A are B, so no J are A."
4 "All B are J, no A are B, so some J are not A."
5 "Some B are J, no A are B, so some J are not A."
6 "Some B are not J, all A are B, so some J are not A."
7 "All B are J, some A are not B, so some J are not A."
8 "No B are J, some A are B, so some J are not A."

The early scholars confined Form IV's productive modes to the first five, and mentioned disagreement over their productivity in syllogisms with two simple premises. We mitigate their disagreement by placing a condition that one of its two particulars be negative.

CONDITIONAL CONNECTING SYLLOGISMS

فصلٌ: في الاقترانيّاتِ مِن الشرطيّةِ

وحالُها في انعقادِ (٦٠) الأشكالِ الأربعةِ، والضروبِ المنتجةِ، والشرائطِ المعتبرةِ، كحالِ (د١٣٩) الاقترانيّاتِ مِن الحمليّاتِ سواءٌ بسواءٍ. (م٦٠)

Their formation in the four figures, the productive moods, and the relevant conditions are identical to those of predicating connecting syllogisms in every respect.

مثالُ الشكلِ الأوّلِ في المتّصلةِ: «كلّما كانَ زيدٌ إنسانًا كانَ حيوانًا، وكلّما كانَ حيوانًا كانَ جسمًا»، ينتجُ: «كلّما كانَ زيدٌ إنسانًا كانَ جسمًا». (ب٨٠)

An example of the first figure for conjunctives is: "Whenever Zaid is a human, he is an animal; whenever he is an animal, he is a body; thus whenever Zaid is a human, he is a body."

مثالُ الشكلِ الثاني: «كلّما كانَ زيدٌ إنسانًا كانَ حيوانًا، وليسَ البتّةَ إذا كانَ حجرًا كانَ حيوانًا»، ينتجُ: «ليسَ البتّةَ إنْ كانَ زيدٌ إنسانًا كانَ حجرًا».

An example of the second figure is: "Whenever Zaid is a human, he is an animal; it is never at all that if he is a stone, he is an animal; thus it is never at all that if Zaid is a human, he is a stone."

مثالُ الثالثِ مِنْها: «كلّما كانَ زيدٌ إنسانًا كانَ حيوانًا، وكلّما كانَ زيدٌ إنسانًا كانَ كاتبًا»، ينتجُ: «قد يكونُ إذا كانَ زيدٌ حيوانًا كانَ كاتبًا».

An example of the third figure is: "Whenever Zaid is a human, he is an animal; whenever Zaid is a human, he is a writer; thus it is possible that if Zaid is an animal, he is a writer."

وأمّا الاقترانيُّ الشرطيُّ المؤلَّفُ مِن منفصلاتٍ فمثالُه مِن الشـكلِ الأوَّلِ: ‹د ١٤٠› «إمّا كلُّ أ ب أو كلُّ ج د، ودائمًا كلّ د هـ أو كلُّ د ز»، ينتجُ: «دائمًا إمّا كلُّ أ ب أو كلُّ ج هـ أو كلُّ د ز».

As for conditional connecting syllogisms composed of disjunctives, an example from the first figure is: "Either every A is B or every J is D; always, every D is H or every D is Z; thus always, either every A is B or every J is H or every D is Z."

وأمّا الاقترانيُّ الشرطيُّ المركّبُ مِن حمليّةٍ ومتّصلةٍ فكقولِنا: «كلَّما كانَ ب ج فكلّ ج أ وكلّ أ هـ»، ينتـجُ: «كلَّمـا كانَ ب ج فكلُّ ج هـ(٦١)» وعلىٰ هذا القياسِ باقي التركيباتِ.

As for conditional connecting syllogisms composed of predicating propositions and conjunctives, an example is: "Whenever B is J, then every J is A; every A is H; thus whenever B is J, then every J is H." The same applies to the remaining compositions.

<table>
<tr><td></td><td>فصلٌ: [في] القياسِ الاستثنائيِّ</td></tr>
</table>

وهو مركّبٌ مِن مقدّمتَينِ، أي: قضيّتَينِ، إحداهما شرطيّةٌ والأخرىٰ حمليّةٌ، ويتخلّلُ بينَهما كلمةُ الاسـتثناءِ، أعني: إلّا وأخواتُها؛ ومِن ثَمَّ يُسمّىٰ: ‹م ٦١› «استثنائيًّا».

---

61   Each edition has something slightly different. Page 83 of the matn-only edition: كلَّما كانَ ب ج فكل ج أ وكلّ أ هـ، ينتجُ: «كلَّما كانَ ب ج فكل ج أ page 81 of the one with commentary: كلَّما كانَ ب ج فكل ج أ وكلّ ء آ، ينتجُ: «كلَّما كانَ ب ج فكل ج أ page 61 of the al-Madīnah edition: كلَّما كانَ ب ج فكل ج أ وكلّ ا ء، ينتجُ: «كلَّما The latter two agree in meaning, so I adjusted the first one كانَ ب ج فكل ج ء to agree with them.

The *excepting syllogism* (*qiyās istithnā'ī*) is composed of two premises (i.e. two propositions) – one conditional and the other predicating – with an exception phrase (i.e. "except" (*illā*) and its equivalents) between them. This structure gives it the name "excepting" (*istithnā'iyyah*).

فإنْ كانتْ الشرطيّةُ متّصلةً فاستثناءُ عينِ المقدّم ينتجُ عينَ التالي، (د١٤١) واستثناءُ نقيضِ التالي ينتجُ رفعَ المقدّمِ، كما تقولُ: «كلَّما كانتْ الشمسُ طالعةً كانَ (ب٨١) النهارُ موجودًا، لكنَّ الشمسَ طالعةٌ»، ينتجُ: «فالنهارُ موجودٌ»، «لكنَّ النهارَ ليسَ بموجودٍ» ينتجُ: «فالشمسُ ليستْ طالعةً».

If the conditional is conjunctive, then excepting the antecedent results in affirming the consequent itself, while excepting the contradictory of the consequent results in denying the antecedent – for example, "Whenever the sun is risen, it is daytime; but the sun is risen; thus it is daytime," and "Whenever the sun is risen, it is daytime; but daytime does not exist; thus the sun is not risen."

وإنْ كانتْ منفصلةً حقيقيّةً فاستثناءُ عينِ أحدِهما ينتجُ نقيضَ الآخرِ وبالعكسِ.

If the conditional premise is a proper disjoining,[62] then excepting one of the parts results in the contradictory of the other, and vice versa.[63]

وفي مانعةِ الجمعِ ينتجُ القسمَ الأوّلَ دونَ الثاني.

---

62   See page 68.

63   For example, our statement: "A number is either even or odd." produces four possible conclusions:

       1. "But it is even. Thus, it is not odd."

       2. "But it is odd. Thus, it is not even."

       3. "But it is not even. Thus, it is odd."

       4. "But it is not odd. Thus, it is even." Cf. Dār al-Malik edition, 142.

In an excluder of conjunction (*māni'at al-jam'*), it produces the first part but denies the second.[64]

وفي مانعةِ الخلوِّ ينتجُ الثاني دونَ الأوّلِ. ‹د١٤٢›

In an excluder of vacuity (*māni'at al-khuluww*), it produces the second part but denies the first.[65]

✳ ✳ ✳

وها هنا قد انتهتْ مباحثُ القياسِ بالقولِ المجملِ، والتفصيلُ موكّولٌ إلى الكتبِ الطوالِ. والآنَ نذكرُ طرفًا مِن لواحقِ القياسِ. ‹م٦٢›

With this, the discussions on syllogisms in general terms have concluded. Detailed discussions are entrusted to longer texts.

Now, we will mention some supplements to syllogisms.

فصلٌ [في الاستقراءِ]

INDUCTIVE REASONING

«الاستقراءُ»، هو: الحكمُ علىٰ كلٍّ بتتبّع أكثرِ الجزئيّاتِ، كقولِنا: «كلُّ حيوانٍ يحرّكُ فكّه الأسفلَ عندَ المضغِ»؛ لأنّا استقرينا، أي: تتبّعنا الإنسانَ، والفرسَ والبعيرَ والحميرَ والطيورَ والسباعَ فوجدنا كلّها كذلكَ، فحكمنا بعدَ تتبّعِ هذهِ الجزئيّاتِ المستقراةِ أنَّ كلَّ حيوانٍ يحرّكُ فكّه الأسفلَ عندَ المضغِ.

---

64   (Tr:) For example, our statement: "This thing is either a tree or a stone."
- "But it is a tree. Thus, it is not a stone."
- "But it is a stone. Thus, it is not a tree."

Denying one part yields no conclusion: "But it is not a tree" does not entail that it is a stone, since it may be neither.

65   (Tr:) For example, our statement: "Either Zaid is in the sea, or he is not sinking."
- "But Zaid is not in the sea. Thus, he is not sinking."
- "But Zaid is sinking. Thus, he is in the sea."

Affirming one part yields no conclusion: "But Zaid is in the sea" does not entail that he is sinking, since both parts may hold simultaneously.

104

Induction (*al-istiqrāʾ*) is asserting a universal judgement by examining most of its particulars – for example, our statement "Every animal moves its lower jaw when chewing," since an examination of humans, horses, camels, donkeys, birds, and predatory animals reveals that all of them do so, leading us to conclude after studying these particulars that every animal moves its lower jaw while chewing.

والاستقراءُ لا يفيدُ اليقينَ، ﴿ب٨٢﴾، وإنَّما يَحصُلُ الظنُّ الغالبُ، لجوازِ أنْ لا يكونَ جميعُ أفرادِ هذا الكلّيِّ بهذهِ الحالةِ، كما يُقالُ: إنَّ التمساحَ ليسَ على هذهِ الصفةِ، بل يحرّكُ فكَه الأعلى.

However, induction does not provide certainty. Rather, it yields only a preponderant assumption (*ẓann ghālib*), since it is possible that not all members of this universal share the condition – for example, it is said that crocodiles do not have this characteristic but instead move their upper jaw.

ANALOGY   فصل [في التمثيلِ]

«التمثيلُ»، وهو: إثباتُ حكمٍ في جزئيٍّ لوجودِه في جزئيٍّ آخرَ لمعنىً جامعٍ مشتركٍ ﴿د٤٣١﴾ بينَهما، كقولِنا: «العالمُ مؤلَّفٌ، فهو حادثٌ، كالبيتِ».

Analogy (*al-tamthīl*) is affirming a ruling for a particular case because it exists in another particular case due to a shared common meaning (*maʿnan jāmiʿ*) – for example, "The world is a composition; thus it is originated, like a house."

ولهم في إثباتِ أنَّ الأمرَ المشتركَ علّةٌ للحكمِ المذكورِ طرقٌ عديدةٌ مذكورةٌ في الأصولِ، العمدةُ فيها طريقانِ:

In *uṣūl al-fiqh*, scholars have mentioned various approaches for proving that the common meaning serves as the cause (*'illah*) for the ruling. Two methods are relied upon:

أحدُهمـا: الــدورانُ عنـدَ المتأخّريـنَ، والقدمـاءُ كانوا يسمّونها بـ «الطردِ والعكسِ»، وهو: أنْ يدورَ الحكمُ (م٦٣) مع المعنى المشـتركِ وجودًا وعدمًا، أي: إذا وُجِدَ المعنىٰ وُجِدَ الحكمُ، وإذا انتفى المعنىٰ انتفىى الحكـمُ. فالدورانُ دليلٌ علىٰ كونِ المدارِ، أعني: المعنىٰ، علّةً للدائرِ، أي: الحكمِ.

The first is known as *coextensiveness* (*dawrān*) by later scholars, while the earlier scholars called it *concomitance and its negation* (*ṭard wa 'aks*): the ruling's presence and absence are correlated with the presence and absence of the common meaning – if the meaning is present the ruling is present, and if the meaning is absent the ruling is absent. Thus, coextensiveness is evidence that the common meaning is the cause (*'illah*) of the ruling.

الطريـقُ الثاني: «السـبرُ والتقسـيمُ»، وهـو: أنَّهم يعـدّونَ أوصافَ (ب٨٣) الأصـلِ، ثـمَّ يثبتـونَ أنَّ مـا وراءَ المعنى المشـتركِ غيرُ صالحٍ لاقتضـاءِ الحكـمِ، وذلـكَ لوجـودِ تلـكَ الأوصافِ في محـلٍّ آخَرَ مع تخلّفِ الحكمِ عنه.

مثلًا في المثالِ المذكورِ يقولونَ: إنَّ علّةَ حدوثِ البيتِ إمّا الإمكانُ (د٤٤١) أو الوجودُ أو الجوهريّةُ أو الجسميّةُ أو التأليفُ. ولا شيءَ مِن المذكـوراتِ غيـرُ التأليفِ بصالحٍ لكونِه علّةً للحدوثِ؛ وإلّا لكانَ كلُّ مكمـنٍ، وكلُّ جوهـرٍ، وكلُّ موجودٍ، وكلُّ (م٦٤) جسـمٍ حادثًا، مع أنَّ الواجبَ تعالىٰ، والجواهرَ المجرّدةَ، والأجسامَ الأثيريّةَ ليستْ كذلكَ.

The second method is *elimination and classification (sabr wa taqsīm).*[66] This method involves identifying the attributes of the original case and demonstrating that none, apart from the common meaning, can serve as the cause for the ruling. This is done by showing that these attributes exist in other cases where the ruling does not follow.

For example, in the house-origination example, they say that the cause of the house's origination must be one of the following: possibility (*imkān*), existence (*wujūd*), substantiality (*jawhari-yyah*), corporeality (*jismiyyah*), or composition (*ta'līf*). None of these except composition is suitable as a cause for origination – otherwise it would follow that every contingent being, every substance, every existent, and every body is originated, whereas the Necessary Being (Most High is He), immaterial substances, and ethereal bodies are not originated.[67]

SYLLOGISM BY WAY OF ABSURDITY (REDUCTIO AD ABSURDUM)

فصلٌ [قياسُ الخُلفِ]

مِن الأقيسـةِ المركّبةِ قياسٌ يُسـمّىٰ: «قياسَ الخُلفِ»، ومرجعُه إلىٰ قياسَينِ.

Among the composite syllogisms is a syllogism called the *syllogism by way of absurdity (qiyās al-khulf*, reductio ad absurdum). Its reduction is to two syllogisms.

أحدُهما: (دد ١٤٥٠) اقترانيٌّ شرطيٌّ مركّبٌ مِن المتصلتَينِ.

The first is a connecting conditional syllogism composed of two conjunctives.

---

66   (Tr:) Or: process of elimination.

67   These three exceptions are according to the philosophers. According to the theologians (*mutakallimūn*), Allah (Most High) is the only exception. See al-Madīnah edition, 65 fn 1; and al-Bushrā edition, 84.

وثانيهما: استثنائيٌّ إحدىٰ مقدّمتَيه لزوميّةٌ، (ب٨٤) أعني: نتيجةُ القياسِ الأوّل، والمقدّمةُ الأخرىٰ مِمّا استثني فيه نقيضُ التالي.

The second is an excepting syllogism; one of its premises is implicative (i.e. the conclusion of the first syllogism), while the other premise is the one in which the contradictory of the consequent is excepted.

تقريرُهُ أنْ يُقـالَ: «المدّعىٰ ثابتٌ؛ لأنّه لو لم يثبتْ المدّعىٰ يثبتُ نقيضُـه، وكلّمـا يثبـتُ نقيضُـه يثبتُ المحـالُ»، ينتجُ: «لـو لم يثبتْ المدّعـىٰ يثبتُ المحـالُ»، وهـذا أوّلُ القياسَـين. ثمّ نجعلُ النتيجةَ المذكورةَ صغرىٰ ونقولُ: «لو لم يثبتْ المدّعىٰ ثبتَ المحالُ»، ونضمُّ إليـه كبرىٰ اسـتثنائيّةً ونقولُ: «لكـنَّ المحالَ ليسَ بثابـتٍ، فبالضرورةِ ثبتَ المدّعىٰ؛ وإلّا لزمَ ارتفاعُ النقيضَينِ».

Its reasoning is expressed as follows: "The claim is affirmed because, if it were not, its contradictory would hold; and whenever its contradictory holds, the impossible follows; thus if the claim is not affirmed, the impossible follows." This is the first syllogism.

Taking this conclusion as the minor premise and adding an excepting major premise: "If the claim is not affirmed, the impossible follows; but the impossible does not hold; thus by necessity, the claim is affirmed – otherwise it would necessitate the simultaneous negation of the two contradictories."

وإنْ اشـتهيتَ فهمَ هذا المعنىٰ في مثالٍ جزئيٍّ نقولُ: «كلُّ إنسـانٍ حيـوانٌ» صـادق؛ لأنّـه لو لـم يصدقْ لصـدقَ «بعضُ الإنسانِ ليسَ بحيـوانٍ»، وكلّمـا صدقَ «بعضُ الإنسـانِ ليـسَ بحيوانٍ» لزمَ المحالُ، ينتـجُ: «كلّمـا لـم يصدقْ المدّعىٰ لـزمَ المحالُ، لكـنَّ المحالَ ليسَ بثابتٍ، فعدمُ ثبوتِ المدّعىٰ ليسَ بثابتٍ، فالمدّعىٰ ثابتٌ»(٦٨). (م٦٥)

---

68   So far, only al-Bushrā edition provides a closing quotation mark. No closing quotation mark is given in al-Madīnah edition; and *Sharḥ al-mirqāt*, 669.

To understand this through a particular example: "'Every human is an animal' is true because, if it were not, 'Some human is not an animal' would be true; and whenever 'Some human is not an animal' is true, the impossible follows; thus whenever the claim is not affirmed, the impossible follows; but the impossible does not hold; thus the non-establishment of the claim does not hold; thus the claim is established."

فصلٌ [لا بدَّ لكلِّ قياسٍ مِن صورةٍ ومادّةٍ]

EVERY SYLLOGISM MUST HAVE
FORM AND MATTER

وينبغي أَنْ يُعلمَ أَنَّ كلَّ قياسٍ لا بدَّ له مِن صورةٍ ومادّةٍ.

It should be known that every syllogism must have both a form (*ṣūrah*) and matter (*māddah*).

أمّا «الصورةُ»، فهي: الهيئةُ الحاصلةُ مِن ترتيبِ المقدّماتِ، ووضع بعضِها عنـدَ بعضٍ. وقد عرفتَ الأشـكالَ الأربعـةَ المنتجةَ، وعلمتَ شرائطَها في الإنتاجِ. بقي أمرُ المادّةُ.

The *form* (*al-ṣūrah*) is the structure that results from arranging the premises and positioning them in relation to one another.

You have already learned the four productive figures and understood their conditions for productivity. The discussion of matter remains.[69]

والقدمـاءُ، حتى الشـيخ الرئيـس، (ب٨٥) كانوا أشـدَّ اهتماما في تفصيلِ موادِّ الأقيسةِ وتوضيحِها، وأكثرَ اعتناءً عن البحثِ في بسطِها وتنقيحِها؛ ذلـكَ لأنَّ معرفـةَ هـذا أتمُّ فائدةً، وأشـملُ عائـدةً لطالبي الصناعةِ. (د١٤٦)

---

69   (Tr:) These will be explained shortly under the heading of "The First Crafts."

The earlier scholars, including the Eminent Shaykh [Ibn Sīnā], were most diligent in detailing the matter of syllogisms and clarifying it. They placed greater emphasis on investigating and refining it [than on expanding upon its forms, as the later scholars did]. This is because understanding this [i.e. the matter] provides greater benefit and broader utility for those pursuing this craft.

لكنَّ المتأخّرينَ قد طوّلوا الكلامَ في بيانِ صورِ الأقيسةِ، وبسطوا فيها غايةَ البسطِ، سيّما في أقيسةِ الشـرطيّاتِ المتّصلةِ والمنفصلةِ، مع قلّةِ جدوىٰ هذهِ المباحثِ، ورفضوا أمرَ المادّةِ، واقتصروا في بيانِها علـىٰ بيـانِ حـدودِ الصناعاتِ الخمـسِ، ولا أدري أيَّ أمرٍ دعاهم إلىٰ ذلكَ؟! وأيَّ باعثٍ أغراهم هنالكَ؟!

However, the later scholars have prolonged their discussions in clarifying the forms of syllogisms, expanding them to the furthest extent – particularly in conjunctive and disjunctive conditional syllogisms – despite the little practical value of these topics. They dismissed the issue of matter, reducing its explanation to merely defining the Five Crafts (*al-ṣināʿāt al-khams*). I do not know what led them to this, nor what impulse enticed them toward it.

ولا بدَّ للفطنِ اللبيبِ أنْ يهتمَّ بهذهِ المباحثِ الجليلةِ الشأنِ الباهرةِ البرهـانِ (م٦٦) غايةَ الاهتمامِ، (د١٤٧) ويطلبُ ذلكَ المطلبَ العظيمَ والمقصدَ الفخيمَ مِن كتبِ القدماءِ المهرةِ وزُبَرِ الأقدمينَ السحرةِ.

It is imperative for the discerning intellect to engage with these noble discussions, illustrious matters, and dazzling proofs with the utmost attention. One should seek this great pursuit and lofty objective from the books of the skilled ancients and the scrolls of the spellbinding early scholars.

فعليــكَ أيّهـا الولـدَ العزيـزَ أنْ تسـمعَ نصيحتي ولا تنـسَ وصيّتي .
وإنّمـا ألقـي عليكَ نبذًا مِمّا يتعلّقُ بهذهِ الصناعاتِ متوكّلًا علىٰ كافي
المهماتِ فاستمعْ:

So, dear student, heed my advice and do not neglect my counsel. I shall now give you a brief overview of what pertains to these crafts, placing my trust in the One who suffices for all essential matters. So listen attentively:

THE FIVE CRAFTS [الصناعاتُ الخمسُ]

إنَّ القيـاسَ باعتبارِ المـادّةِ ينقسـمُ إلىٰ أقسـامٍ خمسةٍ، (ب٨٦)
ويُقـالُ ها: الصناعاتُ الخمسُ: أحدُها: البرهانيُّ، والثاني: الجدليُّ،
والثالثُ: الخطابيُّ، والرابعُ: الشعريُّ، والخامسُ: السفسطيُّ .

Syllogism, when considered in terms of its matter (*māddah*), is divided into five types. They are known as the *Five Crafts* (*al-ṣināʿāt al-khams*).

The first is the demonstrative syllogism (*burhān*).
The second is the dialectical (*jadalī*).
The third is the rhetorical (*khiṭābī*).
The fourth is the poetic (*shiʿrī*).
The fifth is the sophistic (*safsaṭī*).

THE DEMONSTRATIVE SYLLOGISM فصلٌ: في البرهانِ وما يتعلّقُ به

اعلمْ أنَّ البرهانَ قياسٌ مؤلّفٌ مِن اليقينيّاتِ بديهيّةً كانتْ أو نظريّةً
منتهيةً إليها، وليسَ (د١٤٨) الأمرُ كما زعمَ أنَّ البرهانَ إنّما يتألّفُ مِن
البديهيّاتِ فحسب .

Know that the *demonstrative syllogism* (*al-burhān*) is a syllogism composed of certain propositions, whether they are self-evident or discursive, provided they ultimately lead to certainty.

It is not as some have claimed: that demonstration consists solely of self-evident propositions.

ثمَّ البديهيّاتُ ستّةٌ: ﴿م٦٧﴾

Self-evident propositions are six.

1. FIRST PRINCIPLES

[الأوّليّاتُ]

أحدُهــا: «الأوّليّــاتُ»، وهــي: قضايـا يجـزمُ العقـلُ فيهـا بمجـرّدِ الالتفاتِ والتصوّرِ ولا يحتاجُ إلى واسـطةٍ، كقولِكَ: «الكلُّ أعظمُ مِن الجزءِ.».

The first category is *first principles* (*awwaliyyāt*): propositions in which the mind reaches certainty merely by attending to them and conceptualising them, without requiring any intermediary – for example, "The whole is greater than the part."

2. INNATE KNOWLEDGE

[الفطريّاتُ]

وثانيهــا: «الفطريّــاتُ»، وهي: مـا يفتقرُ إلى واسـطةٍ غيرِ غائبةٍ عن الذهنِ أصلًا، ويُقالُ هذهِ القضايا: قضايا قياسُها معها، نحو: «الأربعةُ زوجٌ»؛ فإنَّ مَن تصوّرَ مفهومَ الأربعةِ، وتصوّرَ ﴿د١٤٩﴾ مفهومَ الزوج بأنَّه هو الذي ينقسمُ بمتساوينِ حكمَ بداهةً بأنَّ الأربعةَ زوجٌ، ونحوُ قولِنا: «الواحدُ نصفُ الاثنينِ»؛ فإنَّ العقلَ حكمَ به بعدَ أنْ يلاحظَ مفهومَ نصفِ الاثنينِ والواحدِ.

The second category is *innate knowledge* (*fiṭriyyāt*): propositions that require an intermediary, but one that is never absent from the mind. Such propositions are referred to as *propositions whose syllogism accompanies them* (*qaḍāyā qiyāsuhā maʿhā*) – for example, "Four is an even number," since when one conceptualises four and understands even as that which is evenly divisible, the mind immediately affirms it; and "One is half of two," since the mind affirms it immediately upon recognising the concepts *half of two* and *one*.

3. INTUITIVE CAPACITY   **[الحدسيّاتُ]**

وثالثُهــا: «الحدسيّاتُ»، وهي: ظهورُ المبادئِ دفعـةً واحدةً، مِن دونِ ‹ب٨٧› أَنْ يكونَ هناكَ حركةٌ فكريّةٌ.

والفرقُ بينَ الحدسِ والفكرِ أنَّه لا بدَّ في الفكرِ مِن الحركتَينِ للنفسِ، بـخلافِ ‹م٦٨› الحدسِ. فإنَّ الذهنَ بعدَما حصلَ له المطلوبُ بوجهٍ ما يتحرّكُ في المعاني المخزونةِ والمبادئِ المكنونةِ طالبًا لِما يكونُ لها تناسبٌ بالمطلوبِ حتىٰ يجدَ معلوماتٍ مناسبةً له، وهاهنا تمَّ ‹د١٥٠› الحركـةُ الأولىٰ. ثمَّ يرجعُ قَهْقَرىٰ ويتحـرّكُ ثانيًا مرتّبًا لتلكَ المعلوماتِ المخزونةِ التي وجدَها ترتيبًا تدريجيًّا حتىٰ يصلَ إلى المطلوبِ، وتتمَّ الحركةُ الثانيةُ، فمجموعُ هاتَينِ الحركتَينِ يُسمّىٰ بـ «الفكرِ».

The third category is *intuitions* (*ḥadsiyyāt*): principles that become apparent all at once, without requiring any process of mental speculation.

The difference between intuition (*ḥads*) and thought (*fikr*) is that thought requires the self to go through two mental movements, unlike intuition. After the mind has acquired the desired conclusion in some way, it moves among stored meanings and hidden-away principles, searching for those harmonious with the desired conclusion until it finds suitable ones – this completes the first movement. It then retraces its steps and moves again, gradually arranging the stored meanings it has found until it reaches the desired conclusion – this completes the second movement. The sum of these two movements is what is called *thought* (*fikr*).

مثلًا: إذا كنتَ تصوّرتَ «الإنسانَ» بوجهٍ مِن الوجوهِ كـ «الكاتبِ» و «الضاحكِ» مثلًا، ثمَّ صرتَ طالبًا لماهيّةِ الإنسانِ فحرّكتَ ذهنَكَ إلى المعاني التي عندَكَ مخزونةً، فوجدتَ «الحيوانَ» و «الناطقَ» مناسبًا لمطلوبِكَ فتمّتْ الحركةُ الأولىٰ.

ومبدأُها المطلوبُ المعلومُ مِن وجهٍ، ومنتهاها «الحيوانُ الناطقُ».

ثمَّ ترتّبُ «الحيوانَ» و «الناطقَ» بأنْ تُقَدّمَ «الحيوانَ» - الذي هو الجنسُ - (ب٨٨) علىٰ «الناطقِ» - الذي هو الفصلُ -، وتقول: «الحيوانُ الناطقُ».

وهاهنا تنقطعُ الحركةُ الثانيةُ وحَصَلَ المطلوبُ.

For example, when you conceive of *human* in one of its aspects – such as *writing* or *laughing* – and then seek its quiddity, you move your mind toward the meanings stored within it. Finding *animal* and *rational* suitable for your inquiry completes the first movement, whose starting point is the desired concept known from one perspective and whose end is *rational animal*.

You then arrange *animal* and *rational* by placing *animal* – the genus – before *rational* – the differentia – forming the *rational animal*.[70]

---

70   (Tr:) In Arabic, modifiers follow the word they describe, while in English, modifiers precede it. In both cases, the derived concept holds priority over its modifier.

Here, the second movement stops, and the desired conclusion is reached.

وأمّا الحدسُ ففيه انتقالُ الذهنِ مِن المطلوبِ إلى المبادئِ دفعةً، ومِنْها إلى المطلوبِ كذلكَ.

وأكثرُ ما يكونُ الحدسُ عقيبَ الشوقِ والتعبِ وقد يكونُ بدونِها.

As for intuition (*ḥads*), it involves the mind moving from the sought conclusion to the principles all at once, and then from them back to the sought conclusion in the same instant.

Intuition most often occurs following intense longing and exertion, though it can also arise without them.

والناسُ مختلفونَ في الحدسِ.

فمِنْهم مَن هو قوّيُ الحدسِ كثيرُه، يحصلُ له مِن (م٦٩) المطالبِ أكثرُها بالحدسِ، كالمؤيَّدِ بالقوّةِ القدسيّةِ كالحكماءِ والأولياءِ والأنبياءِ.

ومِنْهم مَن هو قليلُ الحدسِ (د١٥١) ضعيفُه.

ومِنْهم مَن لا حدسَ له، كالمنتهي في البلادةِ.

ومِن هذا يُعلمُ أنَّ البداهةَ والنظريّةَ مختلفانِ بالأشخاصِ والأوقاتِ فرُبَّ حدسيٍّ عندَ فاقدِ القوّةِ القدسيّةِ يكونُ نظريًّا وبديهيًّا عندَ صاحبِها.

(م٧٠، ب٨٩)

People differ in their intuitive capacity.

Some possess strong and numerous intuitions, with most of their conclusions arising from intuition – such as those endowed with a sacred faculty, like sages, *awliyāʾ*, and prophets.

Others have few and weak intuitions.

Some entirely lack intuition, such as those at the extreme of dullness.

From this, it is understood that what is self-evident and what is discursive varies among individuals and across time – an intuitive matter may be discursive for one who lacks the sacred faculty, yet self-evident to one who possesses it.[71]

4. PERCEPTUAL JUDGMENTS   [المشاهداتُ]

ورابعُها: «المشاهداتُ»، ‹د١٥٢› وهي: قضايا يُحكمُ فيها بواسطةِ المشاهدةِ والإحسّاسِ.

The fourth category is *perceptual judgments* (*mushāhadāt*). These are propositions in which judgment is made through direct perception and sensation.

وهي تنقسمُ إلىٰ قسمينِ.

They divide into two types.

الأوّلُ: ما شوهدَ بإحدى الحواسِّ الظاهرةِ، وهي خمسٌ: الباصرةُ، والسـامعةُ، والشـامّةُ، والذائقـةُ، واللامسـةُ، ويُسـمّىٰ هـذا القسـمُ بـ «الحسّياتِ».

The first is what is perceived through one of the *external senses* (*ḥawāss ẓāhirah*), which are five: sight, hearing, smell, taste, and touch. This category is called *sensory perceptions* (*ḥissiyyāt*).

والثانـي: مـا أُدركَ بالمدركاتِ مِن الحـواسِّ الباطنةِ التي هي أيضًا خمسٌ.

١. الحسُّ المشتركُ المدركُ ‹م٧١› للصور. ‹د١٥٣›

٢. والخيالُ الذي هو كالخزانةِ لها.

٣. والوهمُ المدركُ للمعاني الشخصيّةِ والجزئيّةِ.

---

71   Such individuals obtain unknowns without theory and reason. See Dār al-Malik edition, 151.

٤. والحافظةُ التي هي خزانةٌ للمعاني الجزئيّةِ. (ب٩٠)

٥. والمتصرّقةُ التي تتصرّفُ في الصورِ والمعاني بالتحليلِ والتركيبِ.

The second is what is perceived through the *internal senses* (*ḥawāss bāṭinah*), which are also five.

1. *Common sense* (*ḥiss mushtarak*), which conceptualises forms.
2. *Imagination* (*al-khayāl*), which serves as a repository for these forms.
3. The *estimative faculty* (*wahm*), which perceives individual and particular meanings.
4. *Memory* (*ḥāfiẓah*), which preserves particular meanings.
5. The *cognitive faculty* (*mutaṣarrifah*), which analyses and synthesises forms and meanings.

ويُسمّىٰ هذا القسمُ بـ «الوجدانياتِ».

This category is called *internal perceptions* (*wijdāniyyāt*).

ومدركاتُ العقلِ الصرفِ - أعني: الكلّيّاتِ - غيرُ مندرجةٍ في هذا القسمِ. (د١٥٤)

The objects of pure intellect – namely, universals – are not included in this category.

مثالُ القسمِ الثاني: كما حكمنا بأنّ لنا جوعًا وعطشًا.

An example of this second category is our judgement that we are hungry or thirsty.

5. EMPIRICAL JUDGMENTS
[التجريبيات]

وخامسُـها: ((التجريبيات))، وهـي: قضايا يحكمُ العقلُ بها بواسطةِ
تكـرارِ المشـاهدةِ وعـدمِ التخلّفِ حكمًـا كلّيًّا، كالحكمِ بأنَّ شـربَ
السقمونيا مسهّلٌ للصفراءِ. ‹م٧٢›

The fifth category is *empirical judgments* (*tajrībiyyāt*), propositions that the mind affirms through repeated observation,
without encountering any exception (*takhalluf*), thereby establishing a universal rule – for example, one asserts that drinking
scammony (*saqmūniyā*) has a laxative effect on bile based on
consistent experience.

6. RECURRENT MASS-TRANSMITTED REPORTS
[المتواتراتُ]

وسادسُـها: المتواتـراتُ، وهـي: قضايا يُحكـمُ بها بواسطةِ إخبارِ
جماعةٍ يحيلُ العقلُ تواطؤَهم على الكذبِ.

The sixth category is *recurrent mass-transmitted reports* (*mu-
tawāturāt*). These are propositions affirmed by the mind through
reports from a group whose collusion upon falsehood is deemed
impossible.

واختلفوا في أقلِّ عددِ هذهِ الجماعةِ، فقيل: أربعةٌ، ‹د١٥٥› وقيلَ:
عشـرةٌ، وقيلَ: أربعونَ، والأُشـبهُ أنَّ هذا العددَ يختلفُ باختلافِ حالِ
الذيـنَ أخبـروه، واختلافِ الواقعةِ، فلا يتعيّنُ عـددٌ. والضابطُ أنْ يبلغَ
إلى حدٍّ يفيدُ اليقينَ.

Scholars differ regarding the minimum number required for
such a group. Some say four, others ten, and still others forty. The
most reasonable position is that this number varies according to the
reliability of the informants and the nature of the event, and thus

no specific number can be determined. The essential requirement is that the transmission reaches a level that produces certainty.

فهذهِ الستّةُ هي مبادئُ البراهينِ، ومقاطعُ الدليلِ، ومنتهى اليقينِ.

These six constitute the foundations of demonstration, the decisive grounds of proof, and the ultimate source of certainty.

فائدةٌ [استعمالُ المقدّماتِ النقليّةِ في القياسِ البرهانيِّ]

BENEFICIAL POINT: TRANSMITTED PREMISES IN THE DEMONSTRATIVE SYLLOGISM

زعـمَ قـومٌ أنَّ المقدّمـاتِ النقليّةِ لا تُسـتعملُ في القيـاسِ البرهانيِّ ظنًّا مِنْهم أنَّ (د٥٦١) النقلَ يتطرّقُ إليه الغلطُ والخطأُ مِن وجوهٍ شتّىٰ فكيفَ يكونُ [مِن] مبادئِ القياسِ البرهانيِّ الذي يفيدُ القطعَ؟!

Some have claimed that transmitted premises should not be used in the demonstrative syllogism (*burhān*), on the assumption that transmission is prone to errors and inaccuracies from multiple angles. How, then, can it be considered one of the principles of demonstration, which provides certainty?

و[الجوابُ] إنَّ هذا الظنَّ إثمٌ؛ لأنَّ النقلَ كثيرًا ما يفيدُ القطعَ إذا روعيَ فيه (ب٩١) شرائطُ، وانضمّ إليه العقلُ.

نَعم لو قيلَ: إنَّ النقلَ الصرفَ بلا اعتبارِ انضمامِ العقلِ معه لا يعتبرُ ولا يفيدُ، كانَ له وجهٌ.

[The answer is that] this assumption is mistaken, since transmission frequently provides certainty when its conditions are observed and reason is joined to it.

Indeed, if it were said that pure transmission, without the conjunction of reason, carries no weight and yields no [certainty], that would have merit.

TYPES OF DEMONSTRATIVE SYLLOGISM

فصلٌ [أقسامُ البرهانِ]

البرهانُ قسمانِ: لِمِّيٌّ، وإِنِّيٌّ.

The demonstrative syllogism (*burhān*) falls into two categories: the why-demonstration (*limmī*) and the that-demonstration (*innī*).

أمَّا «اللِّمِّيُّ»، فهو: الذي يكونُ فيه الأوسطُ[72] علَّةً لثبوتِ (م٧٣) الأكبرِ للأصغرِ في الواقعِ، كما أنَّه واسطةٌ في الحكمِ، فيُسمَّىٰ به لإفادتِه اللمِّيَّةَ والعلِّيَّةَ. (د١٥٧)

The *why-demonstration* (*limmī*) is one wherein the middle term is the cause for establishing the major term for the minor term, in reality, just as it is an intermediary in the judgement. It is given this name because it provides the why-ness (*limmiyyah*) and causation (*'illiyyah*).

وأمَّا «الإِنِّيُّ»، فهو: الذي يكونُ الأوسطُ فيه علَّةً للحكمِ في الذهنِ فقطْ، ولم يكنْ علَّةً في الواقعِ، بل قد يكونُ معلولًا له.

The *that-demonstration* (*innī*) is one wherein the middle term is a cause for the judgement in the mind only. It is not a cause in reality, but rather it may be an effect of it.

مثالُ اللِّمِّيِّ قولُكَ: «زيدٌ محمومٌ؛ لأنَّه متعفِّنُ الأخلاطِ، وكلُّ متعفِّنِ الأخلاطِ محمومٌ، فزيدٌ محمومٌ»، فكمـا أنَّ في هذا القياسِ الأوسطَ علَّةٌ لثبوتِ الحمىٰ لزيدٍ في ذهنِكَ، كذلـكَ هو علَّةٌ لوجودِ الحمىٰ في الواقعِ.

---

72   In al-Madīnah edition: (الأوسط فيه).

An example of the why-demonstration (*limmī*) is your statement: "Zaid is feverish because he has a disorder of the humours;[73] everyone with a disorder of the humours is feverish; thus Zaid is feverish." Just as the middle term in this syllogism is the cause for affirming Zaid's fever in the mind, it is also the cause for the fever's presence in reality.

ومثالُ الإنّـيِّ قولُـكَ: «زيدٌ متعفّـنُ الأخلاطِ؛ لأنّـه محمومٌ، وكلُّ محمومٍ متعفّنُ الأخلاطِ، فزيدٌ متعفّنُ الأخلاطِ». فوجودُ الحمىٰ علّةٌ لثبـوتِ كونِه متعفّـنِ الأخلاطِ في ذهنِكَ، وليسَ علّةً في نفسِ الأمرِ. بل عسىٰ أنْ يكونَ الأمرُ في الواقعِ بالعكسِ. (ب٩٢)

An example of the that-demonstration (*innī*) is: "Zaid is feverish; everyone who is feverish has a disorder of the humours; thus Zaid has a disorder of the humours." The fever's presence is a cause for affirming in the mind that he has a disorder of the humours, but it is not a cause in reality – indeed, in reality it may be the opposite.

فصلٌ [القياسُ الجدليُّ]

DIALECTICAL SYLLOGISMS

«القياسُ الجدليُّ»: قياسٌ مركّبٌ مِن مقدّماتٍ مشهورةٍ، أو مسلّمةٍ عندَ الخصمِ، صادقةً (د١٥٨) كانتْ أو كاذبةً.

---

73   (Tr:) This refers to Greek humourism which was the dominant system of medicine in the West, Middle East, and India – up until the 19th century. According to humourism, four bodily fluids affect human health, behaviour, and personality. Hippocrates (460–370 BC) is usually credited with being the first to write about applying humourism to medicine. He categorised the humours as blood, phlegm, yellow bile, and black bile. Later, Galen (129–200 CE) categorised the humours as hot, cold, wet, and dry. Humourism was adopted and developed by Muslim physicians. Perhaps the best-known example of Muslim writings on the subjects is Ibn Sīnā's *The Canon of Medicine*, which was a standard medical textbook in European universities as late as 1650 CE.

The *dialectical syllogism* (*qiyās jadalī*) is a syllogism composed of premises that are either well-known (*mashhūrāt*) or conceded by the opponent (*musallamāt*), regardless of whether they are true or false.

والأوّلُ: ما تطابقتْ فيه آراءُ قومٍ إمّا لمصلحةٍ عامّةٍ، نحوِ: «العدلُ حسـنٌ، والظلمُ قبيحٌ، وقتلُ السـارقِ واجبٌ»، أو لرقّةٍ قلبيّةٍ كقولِ أهلِ الهنـدِ: «ذبـحُ الحيوانِ مذمـومٌ»، أو انفعالاتٍ خلقيّةٍ أو مزاجيّةٍ؛ فإنَّ للأمزجةِ والعـاداتِ دخلًا عظيمًا في الاعتقـاداتِ، فأصحابُ (م ٧٤) الأمزجةِ الشديدةِ يرونَ الانتظامَ مع أهلِ الشرارةِ حسنًا، وأهلُ الأمزجةِ اللّيّنـةِ يـرونَ العفـوَ خيرًا، ولذلـكَ ترى النـاسَ مختلفينَ فـي العاداتِ والرسومِ.

The first type [well-known premises] refers to cases where people's opinions align, either due to a common benefit – such as "Justice is good," "Injustice is bad," and "Killing the thief is obligatory" – or due to sentiment, as when the people of India say "Slaughtering animals is reprehensible," or due to emotional influences or temperamental dispositions, since temperaments and customs play a significant role in shaping beliefs: those with harsh temperaments tend to consider associating with corrupt people commendable, while those with gentle temperaments tend to view forgiveness as preferable. For this reason, people differ in their customs and social conventions.

ولـكلِّ قـومٍ مشـهوراتٌ خاصّـةٌ بهـم، وكـذا لـكلِّ صناعـةٍ. فمِن مشـهوراتِ النحويّيـنَ: الفاعلُ مرفوعٌ، والمفعـولُ منصوبٌ، والمضافُ إليه مجرورٌ. ومِن مشهوراتِ الأصوليّينِ: الأمرُ للوجوبِ.

Each group of people has its own well-known premises, as does each discipline – for instance, among grammarians it is well-known that the subject (*fā'il*) is in the nominative (*marfū'*), the object (*maf'ūl*) is in the accusative (*manṣūb*), and the genitive complement (*muḍāf ilayhi*) is in the genitive (*majrūr*); and among legal theorists (*uṣūliyyūn*) that a command (*amr*) implies obligation (*wujūb*).

والثاني: ما يؤلَّفُ مِن المسلّماتِ بينَ المتخاصمينَ. (ب٩٣)

The second type – *conceded premises* (*musallamāt*) – refers to premises explicitly granted by both disputants.

وللمشـهوراتِ شبهٌ بالأوّليّاتِ، وتجريدُ الذهنِ وتدقيـقُ النظرِ يفرّقُ بينَهما.

Well-known premises (*mashhūrāt*) bear a resemblance to first principles (*awwaliyyāt*), yet careful abstraction and precise scrutiny distinguish between them.

والغرضُ مِن صناعةِ الجدلِ إلزامُ الخصمِ، أو حفظُ الرأي. (د١٥٩)

The purpose of the art of dialectical reasoning (*ṣinā'at al-jadal*) is either to compel the opponent (*ilzām al-khaṣm*) or to defend one's own view (*ḥifẓ al-ra'y*).

RHETORICAL SYLLOGISMSفصلٌ [القياسُ الخطابيُّ]

«القياسُ الخطابيُّ»: قياسٌ مفيدٌ للظنِّ.

The *rhetorical syllogism* (*qiyās khiṭābī*) is a syllogism that yields assumption.

ومقدّماتُـه مقبولاتٌ مأخـوذاتٌ ممَّن يحسَـنُ (م٧٥) الظنُّ فيهم، كالأوليـاءِ والحكمـاءِ. أمّا المأخـوذاتُ مِن الأنبياءِ عليهـم وعلىٰ نبيِّنا أفضـلُ الصلاةِ والسلامِ فليسـتْ مِن الخطابـةِ؛ لأنَّها إخباراتٌ صادقةٌ مِـن مخبرٍ صـادقٍ دلَّتْ علىٰ صدقِه المعجـزةُ، ولا مجالَ للوهمِ فيها

حتّىٰ يتطرّقُ إليها الوهمُ والخللُ. فالقياسُ المركّبُ مِنْها برهانيٌّ قطعيُّ المقدّماتِ. (ب٩٤، د١٦٠)

Its premises are accepted, derived from trustworthy sources, such as the *awliyā'* and sages.

What is derived from the prophets (may the best peace and blessings be upon them and upon our Prophet) is not considered rhetorical [in nature]. This is because they are truthful pronouncements from a truthful source whose truthfulness was evinced by miracles, and there is no room for supposition in them, rendering them immune to supposition and flaws. Hence, a syllogism assembled from them is a demonstrative syllogism (*qiyās burhānī*) with decisive premises.

أو مظنوناتٌ يُحكمُ بها بسببِ الرجحانِ، ويندرجُ فيها الحدسيّاتِ والتجريبيّاتِ والمتواتراتِ التي لم تبلغْ إلىٰ حدِّ الجزمِ بسببِ عدمِ شعورِ العلّةِ، أو عدمِ بلوغِ عددِ المخبرينَ إلىٰ مبلغِ التواترِ.

Or [its premises are derived] from assumptions (*maznūnāt*), affirmed on account of preponderance – subsumed within these are intuitions, empirical premises, and recurrent mass-transmitted reports that have not reached the level of conviction, either because the cause is not apparent or because the number of transmitters has not reached the threshold of recurrent mass-transmission.

ولهـذهِ الصناعةِ منفعةٌ عظيمةٌ في تنظيمِ أمورِ المعاشِ، وتنسيقِ أحـكامِ المعـادِ، إمّـا باستعمالِها، أو بالاحتـرازِ عنهـا، ولذلكَ [فقد كانَ] كبارُ الحكماءِ يستعملونَ تلكَ الصناعةَ كثيرًا، ويعظّونَ بالكلامِ الخطابـيِّ جمًّـا غفيـرًا. ولا بدَّ أنْ تكونَ المقدّماتُ المستعملةُ فيها مقنعةً للسامعينَ، مفيدةً للواعظينَ. (د١٦١)

This craft has enormous utility in organising worldly affairs and the affairs of the Hereafter (*aḥkām al-maʿād*), whether by employing it or by guarding against it. For this reason, the senior sages frequently used it, preaching to large audiences with rhetorical discourse.

The premises used therein must be convincing to the audience and beneficial for the preachers.

 فصلٌ [القياسُ الشعريُّ]

«القيـاسُ الشـعريُّ»: قيـاسٌ مؤلَّفٌ مِـن المخـيَّلاتِ الصادقـةِ أو الكَاذبـةِ المسـتحيلةِ أو الممكنـةِ، المؤثِّـرةِ في النفسِ قبضًا وبسـطًا. وللنفسِ مطاوعةٌ للتخييْلِ كمطاوعتِها للتصديقِ بل (م٧٦) أشدُّ منه.

والغرضُ مِن هذهِ الصناعةِ أنْ تنفعلَ النفسُ بالترهيبِ والترغيبِ.

The *poetic syllogism* (*qiyās shi'rī*) is a syllogism composed of imaginatives (*mukhayyelāt*) that can be true or false, impossible or possible, and that cause the soul (*nafs*) to be dejected or exhilarated. The soul responds to imaginations just as it responds to assents – indeed, even more fiercely.

The purpose of this art is to influence the soul through frightening and awakening desires.

واشترطَ في الشعرِ أنْ يكونَ الكلامُ جاريًا على قانونِ اللغةِ، مشتملًا على (ب٩٥) استعاراتٍ بديعةٍ رائقةٍ، وتشـبيهاتٍ أنيقةٍ فائقةٍ، بحيثُ يؤثِّرُ في النفسِ تأثيرًا عجيبًا، ويورثُ فرحًا، ويوجبُ ترحًا.

In a poetic syllogism, it is required that the speech follow the rules of language and that it contain beautiful and serene metaphors and elegant and exquisite similes, so that it has a profound impact on the soul, evoking joy and causing sorrow.

ومِـن ثَـمَّ لا يجـوزُ فيه اسـتعمالُ الأوّليّـاتِ الصادقةِ، ويستحسـنُ استعمالُ المخـيّـلاتِ الكاذبـةِ. (د١٦٢) كما قال العـارفُ الگنجوي مخاطبًا لولِدِه وفِلْذَةِ كَبِدِهِ: (م٧٧)

Hence, it is not permissible to use truthful first principles therein. It is actually preferable to use false imaginatives. As an example, the gnostic al-Ganjawī[74] said to his own son:

در شعـر مپیـچ و در فـنِ او * چـون اکذبِ اوسـت احسـنِ او

Do not involve yourself in poetry and its craft, *
for the most fictitious of it is the best of it.

وكقولِ القائلِ يصفُ الخمرَ:

لَهاالبَدرُكَأْسٌ،وَهيَ شمسٌ، يُديرُها * هِلالٌ، وَكَم يَبْدُو إذا مُزِجَتْ نَجمُ (د١٦٣)

And as one poet described wine:[75]

It has the full moon, a cup, and it is the sun circled by *
a crescent moon. How radiant it becomes when mixed
with a star.

وقالَ الشاعرُ:

لا تَعجَبوا مِن بِلـىٰ غِلالَتِـه * قـد زُرَّ أزرارُهُ على القَمَرِ (د١٦٤)

فشبّهَ المحبوبَ بالقمرِ وقالَ: «لا تعجبوا مِن انشقاقِ غلالتِه؛ لأنّه قمرٌ زُرَّ عليه الغلالة، وكلُّ قمرٍ كذلكَ فغلالتُه تنشقُّ»، ينتجُ: «غلالةُ المحبوبِ تنشقُّ».

---

74   Jamāl al-Dīn Abū Muḥammad Ilyās bin Yūsuf bin al-Zakkī, known as Niẓāmī Ganjawī (535–605 AH/1141–1209 CE).

75   al-Madīnah edition indicates this is ʿUmar Ibn al-Fāriḍ, and he was describing the "wine" of knowing Allah [al-maʿrifah].

The poet said:

"Do not be amazed by the tearing of his gown; *
   For his buttons were buttoned on the moon."

He likened the beloved to the moon and argued: "He is a moon on which a gown has been buttoned; every moon like that has its gown split; thus the beloved's gown will split."

وقـد ينتـجُ اجتماعَ النقيضينِ، نحوُ: «أنا مضمـرُ الحوائج (ب٩٦) باللسـانِ، مظهرُهـا بالمدامـعِ، وكلُّ مضمـرِ الحوائـج صامـتٌ، وكلُّ مظهرِها متكلّمٌ»، ينتجُ: «أنا صامتٌ متكلّمٌ».

It can even produce a combination of two contradictories – for example, "I conceal my needs with my tongue and show them with my tear ducts; everyone who conceals their needs is silent, and everyone who shows them speaks; thus I am a silent speaker."

ولا يُشترطُ الوزنُ في الشعرِ عندَ أربابِ الميزانِ، نَعم يفيدُه حسنًا. والـكلامُ الشـعريُّ إذا أُنشـدَ بصـوتٍ طيّـبٍ ازدادَ تأثيرُه فـي النفوسِ، حتـى (م٧٨) ربَّمـا يزيلُ فرطُ البهجةِ العمائمَ عن الرءوسِ. والأوائلُ مِن الحكماءِ اليونانيّينِ كانوا أحرصَ الناسِ على الشعرِ. (د١٦٥)

Metre is not required in poetry according to the masters of the balance [i.e. logic], though it does enhance it. When poetic speech is recited with a melodious voice, it has a greater impact on the soul, so much so that sometimes extreme happiness might even make turbans fall from heads. The ancient Greek philosophers were the most fervent lovers of poetry.

 فصلٌ [القياسُ السفسطيُّ]

«القياسُ السفسطيُّ»، وهو: قياسٌ مركّبٌ مِن الوهميّاتِ الكاذبةِ
المخترعـةِ للوهـمِ، كقياسٍ غيرِ المحسـوسٍ على المحسـوسٍ، نحوُ:
«كلُّ موجـودٍ مشـارٌ إليـه». وللوهميّـاتِ مشـابهةٌ شـديدةٌ بالأوّليّاتِ،
(ب٩٧) ولـولا ردُّ العقـلِ والشـرعِ حُكْـمَ الوهمِ لدامَ الالتبـاسُ بينَهما.
(د١٦٦)

The *sophistic syllogism* (*qiyās safsaṭī*) is a syllogism composed
of delusive premises designed to delude – for example, comparing
the non-sensory to the sensory: "Every existent being is pointed
to." Delusive premises (*wahmiyyāt*) bear a strong resemblance to
first principles, and were it not for reason and religion repelling
the deluded judgement, confusion between them would persist.

أو مِن الكاذبةِ: المشبّهاتُ بالصادقةِ، وهي: قضايا يعتقدُها العقلُ
بأنّها أوّليّةٌ، أو مشـهورةٌ، أو مقبولةٌ، أو مسـلمةٌ، لمكانِ الاشـتباهِ بها
لفظًا أو معنًى فتُوقِعُ في الغلطِ.

Or [it is composed of] falsehoods mimicking truths – propositions that the mind mistakes for being first principles, well-known,
conceded, or accepted, due to their wording or meaning being
deceptively similar, leading to error.

وهـذهِ الصناعةُ كاذبةٌ مموّهةٌ غيرُ نافعةٍ (م٧٩) بالذاتِ، نَعم نافعةٌ
بالعَرَضِ بأنَّ صاحبَها لا يغلطُ ولا يغالطُ، ويقدرُ على أنْ يغالطَ غيرَه،
وأنْ يمتحنَه بها، أو يعانِدَه.

This art is deceitfully false and useless in itself. However, it
can be useful incidentally, as its wielder can avoid being deceived
or mistaken, mislead others into error, test someone with it, or
dispute them with it.

وصاحبُ هذهِ الصناعةِ إنْ قابلَ الحكيمَ يُسمَّىٰ: «سوفسـطائيًّا»، وهـذهِ الصناعـةُ يُقالُ لها: «سفسـطةٌ»، أي: حكمـةٌ مموّهةٌ ملمّعةٌ. وإلّا فيُسمَّىٰ: «مشاغِبيًّا»، وهذهِ «مشاغبةٌ». وعلى التقديرَينِ فصاحبُها غالطٌ لنفسِه، مغالطٌ لغيرِه، وصناعتُه (د١٦٧) مغالطةٌ.

When a practitioner of this craft stands opposite a sage, he is called a *sophist* (*sūfisṭā'ī*), and the craft is called *sophistry* (*safṣatah*) – meaning speciously disguised and embellished wisdom; otherwise, he is called a *troublemaker* (*mushāghibī*), and it is called *wrangling* (*mushāghabah*).

In both cases, its practitioner misleads himself, misleads others, and his craft is fallacious.

وهـي قيـاسٌ فاسـدٌ إمّا مِن جهةِ المادّةِ فقـطْ، أو مِن جهةِ الصورةِ فقطْ، أو كِلَّيهِما.

It is an invalid syllogism, either only in its matter, or only in its form, or in both.

فصلٌ: في أسبابِ الغلطِ

CAUSES OF ERROR

[أسباب الغلط]

اعلمْ أنَّ أسبابَ الغلطِ مع كثرتِها راجعةٌ إلىٰ أمرَينِ: أحدُهما: سوءُ الفهمِ فقطْ. (م٨٠، ب٩٨) وثانيهما اشتباهُ الكواذبِ بالصوادقِ.

Know that the causes of error can be attributed to two main factors.

The first is just misunderstanding.

The second is confusing falsehoods for truths.

والأوّلُ إنَّما يكونُ بسببِ انغماسِ النفسِ في ظلماتِ الوهمِ، حتىٰ يستيقنَ الكواذبَ صادقةً[76]، بل ضروريّةً، نحوُ: «كلُّ ما ليسَ بمبصرٍ ليسَ بجسمٍ، فالهواءُ ليسَ بجسمٍ».

The first occurs because the self becomes immersed in the darkness of delusion until it is convinced that falsehoods are truths or even immediate truths – for example, "Everything that cannot be seen is not a physical body; thus air is not a physical body."

وأمّا الثاني: ففيه تفصيلٌ علىٰ ما سياتي.

As for the second, it has details as will follow.

وقــالَ بعــضُ المحقّقينَ: ترجعُ إلىٰ أمرٍ واحـدٍ وهو عدمُ التمييِّزِ بينَ الشيءٍ وشبهِه فقطْ.

Some critical scholars said that it reduces to a single factor, which is just the failure to distinguish between a thing and its likeness.

FAILING TO DISTINGUISH BETWEEN
A THING AND ITS LIKENESS

فصلٌ [أقسامُ عدمِ التمييِّزِ بينَ الشيءٍ وشبهِه]

عدمُ التمييِّزِ بينَ الشيءٍ وشبهِه ينقسمُ إلىٰ ما يتعلّقُ بالألفاظِ، وإلىٰ ما يتعلّقُ بالمعاني.

Failing to distinguish between a thing and its likeness is divided into what relates to words and what relates to meanings.

القسمُ الأوّلُ - أعني: ما يتعلّقُ بالألفاظِ - قسمانِ.

الأوّلُ: ما يتعلّقُ بالألفاظِ لا مِن جهةِ التركيبِ. (د١٦٨)

والثاني: ما يتعلّقُ بها مِن حيثُ التركيبِ.

---

76   al-Madīnah edition: (صوادق); al-Bushrā edition: (صادقة).

The first division (i.e. what relates to words) consists of two sub-sections.

The first [sub-section] is what relates to words but not with respect to phrasal construction.

The second is what relates to expressions with respect to phrasal construction.

NON-PHRASAL [المتعلّف بالألفاظِ لا من جهة التركيب]

ثمَّ المتعلّقُ بالألفاظِ مِن جهةِ الأوَّلِ قسمانِ.

Then, what relates to expressions with respect to the first [i.e. without considering their structure] falls into two sub-sections.

الأوَّلُ: ما يتعلّقُ بالألفاظِ نفسِها، وذلكَ بأنْ تكونَ الألفاظُ مختلفةً في الدلالةِ فيقعُ فيها الاشـتباهُ فيما هو المرادُ، كالغلطِ الواقع بسـببِ كونِ اللفظِ مشتركًا (ب٩٩)، لفظيًّا بينَ معنيَينِ فأكثرَ، وكونِ أحدِ معانَيه حقيقيًّا والآخرِ مجازيًا، ويندرجُ فيه الاستعارةُ وأمثالُها. وكلُّ ذلكَ يُسمّىٰ بـ «الاشتراكِ اللفظيِّ»، كما تقولُ لعين الماءِ: «هذهِ عينٌ، وكلُّ عينٍ يستضيءُ بهـا العالمُ، فهذهِ العينُ يستضيءُ بها العالمُ». أو تقولُ: «زيدٌ أسدٌ، وكلُّ أسدٍ له مخالبُ، فزيدٌ له مخالبُ». و[سببُ] الغلطِ فـي الأوَّلِ كـونُ لفظِ العين مشـتركًا لفظيًّا بينَ عينِ الماءِ والشـمسِ، وفـي الثاني كونُ إطلاقِ لفظِ الأسـدِ علـىٰ زيدٍ مجازيًّا، وعلى الحيوانِ المفترسِ حقيقيًّا.

The first is what relates to words themselves, where words carry different indications causing confusion about the intended meaning – such as when a word is shared between two or more meanings, or when one of its meanings is literal and the other figurative, including metaphor and similar figures of speech. All of this is called equivocation (*ishtirāk al-lafẓī*).

For example, when said of a spring (*'ayn al-mā'*): "This is an *'ayn*, and every *'ayn* enlightens the world; thus this *'ayn* enlightens the world" – the ambiguity arises because *'ayn* is shared between spring and sun. Or: "Zaid is a lion (*asad*), and every lion has claws; thus Zaid has claws" – the ambiguity arises because *asad* is applied to Zaid figuratively but to the predatory animal literally.

والثاني: ما يتعلّقُ بالألفاظِ بسببِ التصريفِ، كالاشتباهِ الواقعِ في لفظِ مختارٍ؛ فإنَّه إذا كانَ بمعنى الفاعلِ كانَ أصلُه «مختيرًا» بكسرِ الياءِ. وإذا كانَ بمعنى المفعولِ كانَ أصلُه «مختيَرًا» بفتحها. ‏(د١٦٩)‏ وبسببِ الإعجامِ والإعرابِ، كما يقولُ القائلُ: «غلام حسن»، مِن غيرِ ‏(م٨١)‏ إعرابٍ، فيظنُّ تارةً تركيبًا توصيفيًّا، وأخرىٰ ‏(ب١٠٠)‏ إضافيًّا.

The second is what relates to words due to morphology. Such as the confusion that arises in the word "*mukhtār*" (chosen): if it means the subject, its original form is "*mukhtayir*" (with a *kasrah* under the *yā'*); and if it means the object, its original form is "*mukhtayar*" (with a *fatḥah* over the *yā'*). This confusion also arises due to a lack of diacritical dots and vowel markers (*i'jām wa-i'rāb*)[77] – for instance, someone might say "*ghulām ḥasan*" without any vowel markers, leading to two possible readings: sometimes it is assumed to be a descriptive phrase [i.e. *ghulām ḥasan*, meaning a good boy], and other times a genitive phrase [i.e. *ghulām Ḥasan*, meaning Ḥasan's boy].

PHRASAL ‏[المتعلّف بالألفاظ من جهة التركيب]‏

والمتعلّقُ بالألفاظِ مِن جهةِ التركيبِ فـ ‏(١)‏ إمّـا بالنظرِ إلـى اختلافِ المرجعِ، نحوُ: «مـا يعلمُه الحكيمُ فهـو يعمل بما يعلمُـه»، فإنْ عادَ الضميرُ إلى «الحكيمِ» صدقَ، وإلّا كذبَ. ‏(د١٧٠)‏

---

77   (Tr:) Cf. Amphiboly.

(٢) وإمّا بجمعِ المنفصلِ، نحوُ: «زيدٌ طبيبٌ وماهرٌ» صدقَ، وإن جُمِعَ وقيلَ: «طبيبٌ ماهرٌ» كذبَ.

(٣) وإمّا بإفرادِ المركّبِ، نحوُ: «النارنجُ حلوٌ حامضٌ» صادقٌ، وإن أُفرِدَ وقيلَ: «هذا حلوٌ وحامضٌ» لم يصدقْ.

What[ever] relates to words from the perspective of their structure is either:

1. By considering the reference. For example: "What the wise person knows, he acts upon what he knows," where, if the pronoun

   refers to "the wise person," it is truthful; otherwise, it is false.
2. By combining what is separate.[78] For example: "Zaid is a doctor and skilled" is true, but if combined and stated as: "a skilled doctor," it is false.
3. By separating what is combined.[79] For example: "Seville orange is sweet and sour" is true, but if separated and stated as: "This is sweet and sour," it would not be true.

فصلٌ: في الأغاليطِ التي تقعُ بسببِ المعنىٰ

وهذهِ أيضًا أقسامٌ؛ لأنَّها إمّا مِن جهةِ المادّةِ، أو مِن جهةِ الصورةِ.

This also has divisions, since it can stem from either the direction of the matter, or the form.

أمّا التي مِن جهةِ المادّةِ فكما يكونُ بحيثُ إذا رُتِّبَ المعاني فيه علىٰ وجهٍ يكونُ صادقًا لم يكنْ قياسًا، وإذا رُتِّبَ علىٰ وجهٍ يكونُ قياسًا لم يكنْ صادقًا، كقولِكَ: «الإنسانُ ناطقٌ مِن حيثُ (م٨٢) هو

---

78   (Tr:) Cf. Fallacy of composition, or Combination of words.
79   (Tr:) Cf. Fallacy of division, or division of words.

ناطِقٌ، ‹ب١٠١›، ولا شـيءَ مِن الناطقِ مِن حيـثُ هو ناطقٌ بحيوانٍ، فلا شيءَ مِن الإنسانِ بحيوانٍ». إذْ مع اعتبارِ قيدِ ‹د١٧١› «مِن حيثُ هـو ناطـق» تكذبُ الصغرىٰ، ومع حذفِه عنها تكـذبُ الكبرىٰ، وإنْ حُذِفَ مِن الصغرىٰ وأُثبتَ في الكبرىٰ يلزمُ اختلالُ هيئةِ القياسِ لعدمِ الاشتراكِ.

What arises from the direction of the matter (*māddah*) is such that when the meanings are arranged in a way that is true, it is not a syllogism; and when arranged as a syllogism, it is not true – for example, "A human is a rational being with respect to his being rational; no rational being with respect to his being rational is an animal; thus no human is an animal." For when the restrictive clause "with respect to his being rational" is retained, the minor premise is false; when it is removed from the minor premise, the major premise becomes false; and if it is removed from the minor premise but retained in the major, the syllogism's structure is vitiated by lack of commonality.

وأمّـا التـي مِـن جهةِ الصـورةِ فكما يكونُ علـىٰ هيئةٍ غيـرِ ناتجةٍ، ويجمعُ ذلكَ سوءُ التأليفِ، كقولِ القائلِ: «الزمانُ محيطٌ بالحوادثِ، والفلـكُ محيـطٌ بها أيضًـا»، ينتجُ: «فالزمانُ هو الفلكُ». وهو شـكلٌ ثانٍ، وقد فاتَ فيه شـرطُ اختلافِ المقدّمتَينِ إيجابًا وسـلبًا؛ لكونِهما موجبتَينِ هاهنا.

What arises from the direction of form (*ṣūrah*) is such as when it is in a non-productive form, and all of which falls under poor composition (*sū' al-ta'līf*) – for example, "Time encompasses events; the celestial sphere also encompasses them; thus time is the celestial sphere." This is a second-figure syllogism that fails the condition requiring the two premises to differ in quality, since both are affirmative here.

 [المغالطاتِ التي تقعُ بسببِ فسادِ الصورةِ]

والآنَ نذكـرُ بعـضَ المغالطـاتِ التي سـببُ وقوعِها فسـادُ الصورةِ
فنقولُ:

We shall now mention some of the fallacies that result from a corruption of the form.

So, we say:

(١) مِـن المغالطـاتِ الصوريّـةِ: المصادرةُ علـى المطلوبِ، نحوُ:
«زيدٌ إنسانٌ؛ لأنّه (د١٧٢) بشرٌ، وكلُّ بشرٍ إنسانٌ».

(1) Formal fallacies include *pre-positing the sought conclusion*[80] – for example, "Zaid is a human because he is a man; every man is a human."

(٢) ومِنْها: أخذُ ما بالعَرَضِ مكانَ ما بالذاتِ، نحوُ: «الجالسُ في
السفينةِ متحرّكٌ، وكلُّ متحرّكٍ لا ينبتُ في موضعٍ واحدٍ». (ب١٠٢)

(2) They include *confusing the accidental with the essential* – for example, "Someone sitting on a ship is in motion; every moving entity does not remain in a single place."[81]

(٣) ومِنْها: أنْ لا يتكرّرَ الأوسطُ بتمامِه، كما يُقالُ: «الإنسانُ له
شـعرٌ، وكلُّ شعرٍ ينبتُ»، ينتجُ: «الإنسـانُ ينبتُ»، فإنَّ الأوسطَ «له
شعرٌ» ولم يجعلْ بتمامِه موضوعَ الكبرىٰ.

(3) They include *failure to repeat the middle term in its entirety*[82] – for example, "A human has hair; every hair grows; thus a

---

80   (Tr:) Also known as begging the question and petitio principii.

81   The motion in the minor premise is accidental, while the motion in the major premise is essential. So the middle term has not been repeated, resulting in the form being invalid. Cf. al-Bushrā edition, 102.

82   Cf. Fallacy of the undistributed middle.

human grows," where the middle term is "has hair" but only "hair" is made the subject of the major premise.

(٤) ومِنْها: أنْ لا يكونَ الأوسطُ متشابهًا في المقدّمتَينِ؛ لاختلافِه بالقوّةِ والفعلِ، (د١٧٣) نحوُ قولِه: «السـاكتُ متكلّمٌ، والمتكلّمُ ليسَ بساكتٍ»، ينتجُ: «الساكتُ ليسَ بساكتٍ».

(4) They include *the middle term differing in meaning across the premises due to a distinction between potentiality and actuality* – for example, "The silent one is speaking; the one speaking is not silent; thus the silent one is not silent."

(٥) ومِنْهـا: اخـتلالُ التركيـبِ بسببِ شـكٍّ وقعَ بأنَّ القيـدَ مِن الموضوعِ أو مِن المحمولِ، كقولِهم: «الإنسـانُ وحدَه ضاحكٌ، وكلُّ ضاحـكٍ حيوانٌ»، ينتجُ: «الإنسـانُ وحدَه حيـوانٌ». والغلطُ إنَّما نشأ مِـن توهّـمِ أنَّ لفظـةَ «وحدَه» جـزءٌ مِن الموضـوعِ، ولو جُعـلَ جزءًا مِـن المحمـولِ وقيـلَ: (م٨٣) «الإنسـانُ هو وحدَه ضاحـكٌ، وكلُّ ما هـو وحـدَه ضاحـكٌ فهو حيوانٌ»، لصدقـتْ النتيجةُ؛ لأنَّهـا إذْ ذاكَ: «الإنسان حيوانٌ»، فالغلطُ في هذا المثالِ سوءُ اعتبارِ الحملِ.

(5) They include *a faulty structure due to uncertainty about whether the qualifier belongs to the subject or the predicate* – for example, "The human alone is laughing; every laughing entity is an animal; thus the human alone is an animal." The fallacy arises from taking "alone" as part of the subject. Had it been made part of the predicate – "The human is alone-laughing; everything that is alone-laughing is an animal; thus the human is an animal" – the conclusion would be true. The fallacy in this example is thus a misidentification of the logical attribution.

(٦) ومِنْها: أنْ لا يكونَ الأكبرُ محمولًا علىٰ جميعِ أفرادِ الأوسطِ في الكبرىٰ، وذلكَ كما تقولُ: «كلُّ إنسانٍ حيوانٌ، والحيوانُ عامٌّ أو جنسٌ أو مقولٌ علىٰ كثيرينَ مختلفي الحقيقةِ»، فينتجُ: «كلُّ إنسانٍ عـامٌّ أو جنـسٌ أو مقـولٌ علـىٰ كثيرينَ مختلفي الحقيقةِ»، وهو باطلٌ قطعًا، والسببُ في الغلطِ إنَّما هو إهمالُ كلّيّةِ الكبرىٰ؛ إذْ ‹ب١٠٣› الكبرىٰ طبيعيّةٌ فلا يتعدّىٰ الحكمُ. ‹د١٧٤٥›

(6) They include *the major term not being predicated of all instances of the middle term in the major premise* – for example, "Every human is an animal; 'animal' is a general class, a genus, or predicated of a multitude of entities with differing realities; thus every human is a general class, a genus, or predicated of a multitude of entities with differing realities." This is absolutely fallacious, the reason being the neglect of the universality of the major premise: since the major premise is natural,[83] and therefore the judgement is non-transitive.

(٧) ومِنْها: ما يقعُ بسببِ تقدّمِ الروابطِ أو تأخّرِها عن السـلوبِ، وكـذا تقـدّمُ الجهةِ عن السـلوبِ وتأخّرُها عنها، نحوُ: «زيدٌ ليسَ هو بقائمٍ»، و «زيدٌ هو ليسَ بقائمٍ»، و «بالضرورةِ أنْ لا يكونَ»، و «ليسَ بالضـرورةِ أنْ يكـونَ». و «لا يلـزمُ أنْ يكونَ»، و «يلـزمُ أنْ لا يكونَ». وتكثرُ السـلوبُ مِن هذا ‹م٨٤› البابِ؛ فإنَّ مراتبَ الشفعيّةِ كسـلبِ سـلبٍ، وسـلبِ سـلبِ سـلبِ إثباتٌ، والوتريّةُ كسـلبِ سلبِ السلبِ وغيرِها سلبٌ.

(7) They include *what occurs due to misplacing the copula in relation to the negation, as well as misplacing the modality (jihah)*

---

83   See page {naturalproposition}.

in relation to the negation[84] – for example, "Zaid is-not standing" versus "Zaid is not-standing"; "Necessarily, it must not be" versus "It is not necessarily that it be"; "It is not required to be" versus "It is required to not be." Multiple negation is of this type: an even number of negations affirms, while an odd number negates.

(٨) ومِنْهـا: أخـذُ الاعتبـاراتِ الذهنيّةِ والمحمـولاتِ العقليّةِ أمورًا عينيّـةً، كمـا إذا قيـلَ: «إنَّ الإنسـانَ كلّـيٌّ»، فيظنُّ أنَّه فـي الأعيانِ كذلكَ، وليسَ هذا الظنُّ بصوابٍ؛ فإنَّ الكلّيّةَ إنَّما تُعرضُ للأشياءِ في الذهنِ دونَ الخارجِ.

ومِن هذا التحقيقِ تنحلُّ أغلوطةٌ أخرىٰ، وتقريرُها أنْ يُقالَ: «الممتنعُ موجودٌ؛ لأنَّـه إنْ امتنعَ (د١٧٥) شيءٌ فـي الخارجِ لـكانَ (ب١٠٤) امتناعُه حاصلًا في الخارجِ، فيكونُ الممتنعُ موجودًا في الخارجِ، فيلزمُ وجـودُ الممتنعِ»، وهو باطلٌ قطعًا. وجهُ الانحلالِ: أنَّ الامتناعَ اعتبارٌ ذهنـيٌّ لا يلـزمُ مِن اتّصافِ شـيءٍ بـه وجودُه في الخـارجِ، ليلزمَ وجودٌ للمتّصفِ به في الخارجِ.

(8) They include *treating mental abstractions*[85] *and conceptual predications as concrete entities* (umūr 'ayniyyah)[86] – such as when it is said "Human is a universal" and one assumes this applies extra-mentally as well. This assumption is incorrect, since universality pertains to things only in the mind, not in external actuality.

From this a further fallacy is resolved, formulated as follows: "The impossible exists, because if something is impossible ex-

---

84 See page 58.

85 (Tr:) For example: "Origination is an originated being. Every originated being has origination. Thus, origination has origination" since origination is a rational predication taking the status of something extra-mental, and then asserted with origination.

86 (Tr:) Cf. Fallacy of misplaced concreteness.

tra-mentally, its impossibility would be realised in external actuality, and thus the impossible would exist in external actuality" – which is entirely fallacious. The resolution is that impossibility is a mental consideration, and a thing's being characterised by it does not entail its existence in external actuality, nor therefore the existence of the thing so characterised extra-mentally.

(٩) ومِنْها: أخذُ مثالِ الشيءِ مكانَه. كما تقولُ لمثالِ النارِ: «إنَّه نارٌ، وكلُّ نارٍ محرِقةٌ، فهو محرِقٌ».

(9) They include *confusing a thing's likeness for the thing itself*[87] – for example, "This likeness of fire is fire; every fire burns; thus it burns."

وهذا الاشتباهُ هو الذي احتجَّ به المنكرونَ للوجودِ الذهنيِّ، حيثُ قالوا: لو حصلتْ الأشياءُ ‹م٨٥› بأنفسِها لزِمَ ‹ب٥ ١٠› احتراقُ الذهنِ عندَ وجودِ النارِ، واختراقُه عندَ تصوّرِ الجبلِ، واتّصافِه بالبياضِ والسوادِ عندِ تصوّرِهما، وهكذا.

وحلُّه: أنّه مِن بـابِ أخذِ ما بالعَرَضِ مكانَ ما بالذاتِ، يعني: أنَّ الاحتـراقَ والخـرقَ وغيرَهمـا مِن العوارضِ ‹د١٧٦› التي تلحقُ الشـيءَ إذا وُجـدَ بوجودٍ أصليٍّ خارجيٍّ، وليستْ مِـن العوارضِ للوجودِ الظلّيِّ الذهنيِّ.

This confusion is what rejectors of mental existence use as an argument: if things existed in the mind as they are in themselves, the mind would necessarily burn upon conceiving fire, be torn upon conceiving a mountain, and be attributed with whiteness and blackness upon conceiving them – and so on. The resolution is that this falls under the aforementioned category of confusing the accidental with the essential: burning, tearing, and similar

---

87   (Tr:) Cf. Fallacy of reification.

attributes accompany a thing only when it has external, substantial existence, and are not attributes of its ephemeral mental existence.[88]

(١٠) ومِنْها: أخــذُ جزءِ العلّةِ مكانَ العلّةِ، كما إذا حملَ سبعونَ رجلًا حجرًا ثقيلًا سبعينَ فرسخًا مثلًا، فيتوّهمُ أنَّ الواحدَ مِنْهم يحملُه فرسخًا واحدًا.

(10) They include *mistaking part of the cause for the whole cause* – for example, when seventy men carried a heavy stone seventy *farsakh* [slightly over 354 kilometres or 218.75 miles], and one mistakenly thinks that each carried it a single *farsakh*.

(١١) ومِنْهـا: إجراءُ طريقٍ [89] الأوّلويّةِ عندَ الاختلافِ، كما تقولُ: «الإنسانُ ليسَ بأولىٰ بإضافةِ النفسِ الناطقةِ مِن العصفورِ بعدَ ما اشتركا في الحيوانيّةِ». (م٨٦، د١٧٧٥)

(11) They include *applying the principle of priority in cases of essential disagreement* – for example, "A human is not more entitled to possess the attribute 'rational self' than a sparrow, since they both share animality."

(١٢) ومِنْها: ما يقعُ مِن قلّةِ المبالاةِ بالحيثيّاتِ وتركِ الاعتناءِ بها، كقــولِ القائــلِ: «كلُّ أبيــضَ داخلٌ في حقيقتِه البيـاضُ، وزيدٌ أبيضُ، فيلزمُ دخولُ البياضِ في حقيقتِه».
ومِنـشأُ الغلـطُ فيه: أنَّ البياضَ داخلٌ في مفهومِ الأبيضِ مِن حيثُ إنّه أبيضُ، لا مِن حيثُ إنّه حيوانٌ و إنسانٌ.

---

88 Cf. al-Bushrā edition, p 106; al-Madīnah edition, p86 fn 1.

89 al-Bushrā edition: (إجراءُ طريقٍ); al-Madīnah edition: (إجراءُ طيقٍ), apparently a misprint for (طيقٍ).

(12) They include *what arises from a lack of concern for conceptual considerations (ḥaythiyyāt) and ignoring them*[90] – for example, "Every white thing has whiteness within its quiddity; Zaid is white; thus whiteness must be within his quiddity." The source of the mistake is that whiteness falls within the concept of being white insofar as it is white, not insofar as it is an animal or a human.

(١٣) وِمِنْها قولُهم: مماثلُ المماثلِ مماثلٌ، نحوُ: «الإنسانُ مماثلُ النخلةِ، والنخلةُ ماثلةٌ للحجرِ في كونه غيرَ ذي نفسٍ، فيلزمُ كونَ زيدٍ جمادًا».

ووجهُ التغليطِ: أنَّ مماثلتَها للإنسانِ في أمرٍ، وهو الطولُ مثلًا، ومماثلتُها (ب١٠٦) للحجرِ في شيءٍ آخرَ.

(13) They include *the claim that the like of a like is a like* – for example, "A human is similar to a date palm; a date palm is similar to a stone in lacking ensoulment; thus Zaid is an inanimate." The mistake is that the palm's similarity to the human is in one respect (height, for example), while its similarity to the stone is in another.

(١٤) وِممَّا يوقعُ في الغلطِ: أخذُ العدمِ المقابلِ للملكةِ مكانَ الضدِّ والنقيضِ، كالسكونِ فإنَّه عدمُ الحركةِ عمّا مِن شأنِه أنْ يتحرّكَ، وكالعمىٰ فإنَّه عدمُ البصرِ عمّا مِن شأنِه أنْ يكونَ بصيرًا؛ فيظنُّ أنَّ المجرّدَ ساكنةٌ، والجدارَ أعمىٰ.

(14) Among what leads to error is *confusing a privative absence for a contrary (ḍidd) or the contradictory (naqīḍ)* – for example, stillness, which is the absence of motion in what is capable of motion, and blindness, which is the absence of sight in what is

---

90   (Tr:) Cf. Category Error, and Misunderstanding of Quiddity.

capable of sight; leading one to assume that a non-embodied
entity is still and that a wall is blind.

(١٥) ومِن المغالطاتِ المشهورةِ: قولُهم: لا يمكنُ تحصيلُ
مجهولٍ؛ لأنَّ ذلكَ المجهولَ إذْ حصلَ فبما تعرفُ أنَّه مطلوبُكَ؟ فلا
بـدَّ مِن بقاءِ الجهلِ أو وجودِ العلمِ قبلَه حتىٰ ‹د١٧٨› تعرفَ أنَّه هو،
وعلى التقديرَينِ يمتنعُ تحصيلُه. أمّا على الأوَّلِ: فلاستحالةِ معرفتِه إذا
وُجِدَ. وأمّا على الثاني: فلامتناع تحصيلِ الحاصلِ.

والجوابُ: أنَّ المطلوبَ معلومٌ مِن وجهٍ، ومجهولٌ مِن ‹م٨٧› وجهٍ.
فبعدَ حصولِ المجهولِ يعلمُ بالوجهِ المعلومِ المخصّصِ أنَّه المطلوبُ.
وهذا كمثلِ عبدٍ آبقٍ إذا وُجِدَ فإنَّه كانَ معلومُ الذاتِ مجهولَ المكانِ،
فبعدَ ما وُجِدَ عرفتَ بما كنتَ عارفًا به مِن ذاتِه وصورتِه أنَّه آبقُكَ.

(15) Among the famous fallacies is their statement that the
unknown cannot be attained, for if the unknown is attained, how
would one know it is the desired conclusion? Ignorance must therefore either persist, or knowledge must already exist beforehand
so that one may recognise it as the sought conclusion – and on
either supposition, attaining it is impossible: on the first, because
recognising it upon its being found is impossible; on the second,
because acquiring what is already known is impossible.

The response is that the desired conclusion is known from one
aspect and unknown from another. After attaining the unknown,
one recognises it through the known aspect as the desired conclusion – just as with a runaway slave whose identity was known but
whose whereabouts were not: once he is found, one recognises
him through what one already knew of his essence and form as
one's runaway slave.

أغلوطةٌ: لـو لـم تصدقْ قضيّةٌ لم يصـدقْ «زيدٌ قائمٌ»، وكلَّما لم
يصـدقْ «زيـدٌ قائمٌ» صدق نقيضُه، أعني: «زيـدٌ ليسَ بقائمٍ»، ينتجُ:

«كلَّما لـم تصدقْ قضيّةٌ صدقَ صدـقُ ‹زيدٌ ليسَ بقائمٍ› ‹ب١٠٧›، مع أنَّها قضيّةٌ مِن القضايا». ‹د١٨٩›

والحلُّ: أنَّ التقاديرَ المأخوذةَ في الكبرىٰ، أعني قولَكَ: «كلَّما لم يصدقْ ‹زيدٌ قائمٌ› صدقَ نقيضُه، أعني: ‹زيدٌ ليسَ بقائمٍ››»، إنْ كانتْ واقعيّةً فصدقُها مسلَّمٌ، لكنْ لا اندراجَ؛ إذْ الحكمُ في الصغرىٰ - على التقاديرِ الفرضيّةِ الغيرِ الواقعيّةِ ضرورةَ أنَّ عدمَ صدقِ قضيّةٍ مِن القضايا مِـن الممتنعـاتِ، ضـرورةَ أنَّ قولَنـا: «الواجبُ موجودٌ، أو سـميعٌ، أو بصيرٌ» واجبُ الصدقِ؛ فيكونُ عدمُ صدقِها محالًا. ‹د١٨٠›

وإنْ كانتْ تقاديرُ الكبرىٰ أعمَّ منعنا الكلّيّةَ؛ إذْ كذبُ الشيءٍ إنَّما يسـتلزمُ صدقَ نقيضه بحسـبِ الواقع؛ فإنّه جائزٌ علىٰ تقديرِ المحالِ أنْ يكذبَ النقيضانِ معًا؛ لأنَّ المحالَ جازَ أنْ يستلزمَ محالًا آخرَ.

Fallacy: If a proposition is not true, the proposition "Zaid is standing" is not true. Whenever "Zaid is standing" is not true, its contradictory is true (i.e. "Zaid is not standing"). This produces: "Whenever a proposition is not true, 'Zaid is not standing' is true despite it being a proposition."

Solution: If the hypothetical assumptions in the major premise (i.e. your statement: "Whenever 'Zaid is standing' is not true, its contradictory – meaning: 'Zaid is not standing' – is true") were realistic, their truth would be accepted.

However, there is no subsumption [i.e. the minor term is not subsumed under the major term][91] since the judgement in the minor premise is based on unrealistic hypothetical estimations.

---

91   Meaning: if the realistic estimates are considered in the major premise, it is true. But the minor term is not subsumed within the major term since the assertion in the major premise is based on realistic estimates, while in the minor premise it is based on hypothetical and impossible estimates. Cf. al-Bushrā edition, 108.

By necessity, asserting the impossibility of any proposition is impossible, because our statement "The Necessarily-existent exists, or hears, or sees" is necessarily true – so its lack of being true is impossible.[92]

And if the hypothetical assumption of the major premise were more general, we would reject the universality, since asserting something false implies asserting its contradictory as true, according to reality, for it is possible for the absurd to imply another absurdity.

ويقربُ مِن هـذهِ الأغلوطـةِ: المغالطـةُ العامّةُ الـورودِ (م ٨٨) التي يمكـنُ أنْ تثبـتَ بها أيَّ مطلوبٍ أردتَ صادقًا كانَ أو كاذبًا، فتقولُ: «المدّعىٰ ثابتٌ؛ لأنَّـه لو لم يكنْ المدّعىٰ ثابتًا كانَ نقيضُه ثابتًا، وكلَّما كانَ نقيضُه ثابتًا كانَ شيءٌ مِن الأشياءِ ثابتًا»، ينتجُ: «لو لم يكنْ المدّعىٰ ثابتًا كانَ شـيءٌ مِن الأشياءِ ثابتًا». (ب ١٠٨) وبعكسِ النقيضِ: «لو لم يكنْ شيءٌ مِن الأشياءِ ثابتًا كانَ المدّعىٰ ثابتًا مع أنَّه شيءٌ مِن الأشياءِ». هذا خلفٌ.

Close to this fallacy is the universally-circulated fallacy that can be used to affirm any conclusion one wants, whether true or false. One says: the claim is established, because if it were not established its contradictory would be established, and whenever its contradictory is established, something would be established – which produces: if the claim is not established, something would be established. Then by converting the contradictory: if nothing is established, the claim is established, despite it being itself a thing. This is an absurdity.[93]

---

92   Meaning: the lack of any proposition being true is impossible since "the Necessary is existent" is a proposition which is necessarily true. Cf. al-Bushrā edition, 108.

93   See page 107.

تحيّرُ العـقلاءُ فـي حلِّه. فمِـنْ قائلٍ يقـولُ: إنّا لا نسـلِّمُ أنَّ تلكَ الشـرطيّةَ تنعكسُ بهذا العكسِ إلىٰ هذهِ الشرطيّةِ، كيفَ والشيئانِ في الأصـلِ والعكسِ ﴿د١٨١﴾ مختلفـانِ بالعمومِ والخصـوصِ؟ بل عكسُ هذهِ الشـرطيّةِ قولُنا: «كلَّما لم يكنْ ذلكَ الشـيءُ ثابتًا كانَ المدَّعىٰ ثابتًا». وهو حقٌّ.

وإنْ شـئتَ قلتَ بتقريرٍ آخرَ: إنْ عكسَ تلكَ الشـرطيّةُ: لو لم يكنْ شـيءٌ مِن الأشـياءِ ثابتًا في ضمنِ نقيضِ المدَّعىٰ كانَ المدَّعىٰ ثابتًا. ومِن مجيبٍ يجيبُ بأنَّ المقدَّمَ في العكسِ محالٌ، والمحالُ جازَ أنْ يستلزمَ نقيضَه فلا خُلفٌ.

Its resolution perplexes minds. Some say, "We do not accept that this conditional proposition is logically equivalent to its supposed converse. How could it, when the two things in the original and the converse disagree with respect to being general and particular?" Rather, they argue, the converse of this conditional should be: "If that thing is not established, then the claim must be established." And this, they say, is correct.

Alternatively, one might state the argument differently by saying: "The converse of this conditional is: 'If nothing is established within the scope of the contradictory of the claim, then the claim must be established.'"

In response, another might argue that the premise in the conversion is absurd. However, the impossible may entail its contradictory, so this is not an absurdity.[94]

وقـد وقعَ الإطنابُ في تفصيلِ هذا البابِ لِما أنَّ الرسـائلَ المدوّنةَ في هذا الفنِّ التي ﴿د١٨٢﴾ جرّتْ في زمانِ هذا عادةً قراءتُها خاليةٌ مِن

---

94   See page 107.

تفصيلِ بابِ المغالطةِ فرأيتُ أنْ أوشحَ بذكرِه رسالتي هذهِ لتكونَ نافعةً
للمتعلمينَ، مفيدةً للطالبينَ. (ب١٠٩)

The long digression into the details of this topic has occurred because the written treatises in this field circulating in this era are usually read without any elaboration on the topic of fallacies. So I saw it appropriate to include its discussion in this treatise of mine, so it may benefit learners and assist students.

فصلٌ [القياسُ الذي إحدىٰ
NON-DEMONSTRATIVE
SYLLOGISMS
مقدّمتَيه غيرُ برهانيّةٍ]

ولا بدَّ أنْ يعلمَ أنَّه إذا كانتْ إحدىٰ مقدّمتَي القياسِ غيرَ برهانيّةٍ بل
كانتْ جدليّةً، أو خطابيّةً، أو شعريّةً، أو غيرَها كانَ القياسُ أيضًا غيرَ
برهانيٍّ، وكذا الكلامُ في القياسِ الجدليِّ ونظائرِه. وبالجملةِ فالمؤلّفُ
مِن الراجحِ والمرجوحِ مرجوحٌ.

It must be known that when one of the premises of a syllogism is not demonstrative – but rather dialectical, rhetorical, poetic, or otherwise – then the syllogism is also non-demonstrative.

The same principle applies to the dialectical syllogism and its peers.

In summary, a composition made up of both the preponderant and the outweighed is itself outweighed.

* * *

وهاهنــا قــد تـمَّ بحثُ الصناعــاتِ الخمـسِ، وبه تمّتْ مقاصـدُ الفنِّ
بنوعَيـه، أعني: الموصلِ إلى التصوّرِ، والموصلِ إلى التصديقِ. (م٨٩،
ب١١٠)

Here, the discussion of the Five Crafts is complete. With this, the objectives of the discipline have been concluded in both aspects, namely: what leads to conception and what leads to assent.

5

SUPPLEMENTARY MATTERS

خاتمةٌ [في أنَّ لكلِّ علمٍ ثلاثةَ أمورٍ]

خاتمةٌ لكلِّ علمٍ ثلاثةُ أمورٍ.

Every science has three aspects.

[الموضوع]

أحدُها: «الموضوعُ»، وهو: مـا يُبحثُ في العلمِ عـن عوارضِه ولواحقِه الذاتيّةِ، كبدنِ (د١٨٣) الإنسانِ لعلمِ الطبِّ، والكلمةِ والكلامِ لعلـمِ النحوِ، والمقـدارِ المتّصـلِ لعلمِ الهندسـةِ، والمعلـومِ التصوّريِّ والمعلومِ التصديقيِّ لصناعتي هذهِ.

The first is the *subject* (*mawḍūʿ*), which is that whose essential accidents (*ʿawāriḍ dhātiyyah*) and inherent attributes (*lawāḥiq dhātiyyah*) are investigated in the science – such as the human body in medicine, words and speech in grammar, continuous magnitude (*miqdār muttaṣil*) in geometry, and conceptual and assertorial knowledge in these two disciplines.

وينبغـي أنْ يعلمَ أنَّـه لا يُبحثُ عـن وجودِ الموضوعِ، ولا يبحثُ عـن ماهيّتِـه في العلمِ الذي هو موضوعٌ لـه. فلا يبحثُ الطبيبُ عن بدنِ الإنسانِ مِن حيثُ إنّه موجودٌ، أو جسمٌ نامٍ أو حيوانٌ ناطقٌ، ولا النحويُّ عن حقيقةِ الكلمةِ والكلامِ.

It is necessary to know that neither the existence of the subject nor its quiddity (*māhiyyah*) is investigated in the very science in which it is the subject.

Thus, a physician does not investigate the existence of the human body in terms of it being an existent entity, a growing body, or a rational animal. Likewise, a grammarian does not investigate the true reality (*ḥaqīqah*) of words and speech.

ومِن ثَمَّ لمّا كانَ موضوعُ علمِ الطبيعيِّ الجسمَ (د١٨٤) المطلقَ، وكانَ صاحبُ الفنِّ يوردُ مباحثَ الهيولىٰ والصورةِ، أشكلَ عليهِ أنَّ الهيولىٰ والصورةَ مِن أجزاءِ الجسمِ ومقوّماتِهِ، فكيفَ يوردُ هذهِ المباحثَ في الطبيعيّاتِ؟!

واعتذرْ مِن قبلِه بأنَّ هذهِ المباحثَ استطراديّةٌ.

For this reason, when the subject of natural philosophy (*'ilm al-ṭabī'ī*) was defined as body in the absolute sense (*jism muṭlaq*), its master[95] discussed hyle (*haylūlā*) and form (*ṣūrah*).[96]

This led to an objection: hyle and form are among the parts (*ajzā'*) and constituents (*muqawwimāt*) of body – so how can these topics be discussed within natural philosophy (*al-ṭabī'iyyāt*) itself?

This was excused by arguing that such discussions are incidental digressions (*mabāḥith istaṭrādiyyah*).

PRINCIPLES   [المبادئ]

وثانيها: مباديه، و «المبادئُ»: ما يبتني عليه المسائلُ.

The second is its principles. *Principles* (*mabādi'*) are what the issues (*masā'il*) are built upon.

---

95   (Tr:) Most likely a reference to Ibn Sīnā.

96   Hyle (*haylūlā*) is matter which has the potential to take on a particular form. Cf. al-Madīnah edition, 90 fn 2.

وهي إمّا تصوّريّةٌ، أي: حدودٌ تورِدُ لموضوعِ الصناعةِ وأجزائِه وجزئيّاتِه وأعراضِه الذاتيّةِ. أو تصديقيّةٌ وهي: المقدّماتُ التي تؤلَّفُ مِنْها قياساتُه، [وهي] إمّا بديهيّةٌ (ب١١١) وتُسمّىٰ: «العلومَ المتعارفةَ»، أو غيرُ بديهيّةٍ بل نظريّةٌ مسلّمةٌ.

فإنْ كانَ التسليمُ علىٰ سبيلِ حسنِ الظنِّ مِمَّن ألقاهُ إليه تُسمّىٰ: «أصولًا موضوعةً».

فإنْ كانَ التسليمُ مع الاستنكارِ تسمّىٰ: «مصادرةً».

These are either *conceptual* (*taṣawwuriyyah*): definitions (*ḥudūd*) provided for the subject of the discipline, its parts, particulars, and essential accidents (*aʿrāḍ dhātiyyah*); or *assertorial* (*taṣdīqiyyah*): premises (*muqaddimāt*) from which its syllogisms (*qiyāsāt*) are constructed.

These [assertorial] principles are either *self-evident* (*badīhiyyah*), referred to as common knowledge (*ʿulūm mutaʿārifah*); or non-self-evident, but accepted (*musallamah*) which, if they are accepted in good faith from the one who presents them, are called *postulated principles* (*uṣūl mawḍūʿah*), or, if their acceptance is accompanied by resistance, they are called a *postulate* (*muṣādarah*).

[المسائل]

وثالثُها: «المسائلُ»، وهي التي اشتملَ العلمُ عليها ويحاولُ إثباتَها بالدليلِ.

The third is the *issues* (*masāʾil*), which are the propositions contained within a science and sought to be established through proof.

THE EIGHT HEADINGS

فصلٌ [في الرؤوسِ الثمانيةِ]

اعلَمْ أنَّ القدمـاءَ كانـوا يذكرونَ في مبادئِ الكتبِ أشـياءَ ثمانيةً، ويسمّونها: «الرؤوسَ الثمانيةَ». (د١٨٥)

Know that the ancients would mention eight things at the beginning of books, calling them *The Eight Headings* (*al-ru'ūs al-thamāniyah*).

أحدُها: «الغرضُ»، أعني: العلّةَ الغائيّةَ لئلا يكونَ الناظرُ عابثًا.

وثانيها: «المنفعةُ»؛ لتسهّلَ عليه المشقّةَ في تحصيلِه.

وثالثُها: «التسميةُ»، أعني: عنوانَ العلمِ؛ ليكونَ عندَ الناظرِ إجمالُ ما يُفَصِّلُه الغرضَ. (ب١١٢)

ورابعُها: «المؤلّفُ»؛ ليسكنَ قلبُ المتعلّمِ.

وخامسُـها: أنَّه «في أيِّ مرتبةٍ هـو»؛ ليعلمَ علـى أيِّ علمٍ يجبُ تقديمُه، وعن أيِّ علمٍ يجبُ تأخيرُه. (د١٨٦)

The first is the *purpose* (*gharaḍ*), i.e. the ultimate aim, so the investigator is not aimless.

The second is the *utility* (*manfaʿah*), to ease the difficulty of acquiring it.

The third is the *designation* (*tasmiyah*), that is, the title of the science, so the investigator has an overall picture of what explains the goal in detail.

The fourth is the *author* (*muʾallif*, lit. composer), to settle the student's heart.

The fifth is *its rank*, to know which science precedes it and which follows it.

وسادسُها: أنَّه «مِن أيِّ علمٍ هو»؛ ليطلبَ ما يليقُ به.

وسابعُها: «القسمةُ»، وهي: أبوابُ العلمِ والكتابِ.

وثامِنُها: «أنحاءُ التعليـمِ»، وهـي: التقسـيمُ ‹د١٨٧› والتحليـلُ ‹د١٨٨› والتحديدُ ‹د١٩٠› والبرهانُ؛ ليعرفَ أنَّ الكتابَ مشتملٌ على كلِّها أو بعضِها.

The sixth is *its classification*, so that one may seek what befits it.

The seventh is the *organisation* (*qismah*), which refers to the chapters [i.e. outline] of the science and the book.

The eighth is *modes of instruction* (*anhāʾ al-taʿlīm*): division (*taqsīm*), analysis (*taḥlīl*), delimitation (*taḥdīd*), and demonstration (*burhān*) – so that one may know whether the book encompasses all of these methods or only some.

AUTHOR'S CLOSING REMARKS

[خاتمةُ المؤلِّفِ]

وأقـولُ أنَّـا محمّدٌ فضلُ إمام الخَيْرآبادِيُّ: هـذا آخرُ ما أردنا جمعَه
وتأليفَـه فـي هذهِ الرسـالةِ مِن كتـبِ الأقدمينَ، وكلمـاتِ المتأخّرينَ،
والغرضُ مِن هذا التأليفِ ليسَ إلَّا تعليمُ المبتدئينَ، وتسهيلُ الأمرِ على
الطالبينَ، فإنْ نفعتْكَ أيّها الطالبَ الراغبَ هذهِ العجالةُ نفعًا يسيرًا فلا
تنسني بدعاءِ حسنِ الخاتمةِ، والنجاةَ مِن الحاطمةِ، ﴿ب١١٣﴾ وصلَّى
اللّهُ علىٰ سيّدِنا محمّدٍ خاتمِ النبيّينَ أوّلًا وآخرًا وظاهرًا وباطنًا، والحمدُ
للّهِ ربِّ العالمينَ. ﴿م٩١، ب١١٤، د١٩١٥﴾

And I, Muḥammad Faḍl Imām Khayrābadī, say:

This is the conclusion of what I intended to gather and compile
in this treatise from the books of the ancients and the words of
the later scholars. The purpose of this composition is none other
than to educate beginners and to facilitate learning for students.

If this brief work has benefited you, O aspiring student – even
in the slightest – then do not forget me in your supplications for
a good ending and deliverance from the Demolisher.[97]

May Allah bless our master Muḥammad, the Seal of the Prophets, first and last, manifest and hidden. All praise be to Allah, Lord
of all the Worlds.

❧ END

---

97   (Tr:) i.e. the various hardships and tribulations of death.

BIBLIOGRAPHY

[المَصادِرُ]

al-Abharī, Athīr al-Dīn. *Isagoge: A Classical Primer in Logic.* Translated by Feryal Salem. Chicago: Blue Mountain Press, 2022.

——— , and Zakariyā al-Anṣārī. *Al-Maṭlaʿ Sharḥ Īsāghūjī.* Kuwait: Dār al-Ḍiyāʾ: n.d.

——— , and Ḥusām al-Dīn al-Kātī. *Sharḥ Kitāb Īsāghūjī fī ʿilm al-manṭiq.* Beirut: Dār al-Dhakhāʾir: 1436/2015.

Ibn Sīnā. *Avicenna's Deliverance: Logic.* Translation and notes by Asad Q. Ahmed. Oxford: Oxford University Press, 2011.

Khayrābādī, Faḍl Imām. *Al-Mirqāt.* Edited by ʿAbd al-Raḥmān bin Aḥmad Āl ʿAbd al-Qādīr. n.p.: n.p., c. 1428.

———. *Al-Mirqāt.* Printed with *Al-Mishkāt.* Karachi: Maktabah al-Madīnah, 1436/2015.

———. *Al-Mirqāt.* Printed with Muḥammad ʿImmād al-Dīn al-Shīrkūtī's *Al-Mirʾāh.* Karachi: Maktabat al-Bushrā, 1433/2011.

>———. *Al-Mirqāt.* Printed with Shaykh Muḥammad ʿAbd al-Ḥakīm Sharaf al-Qādūrī's *Al-Mirḍāt.* Bareilly, Uttar Pradesh, India: Dār al-Malik, 1444/2022

——— , and Muḥammad ʿAbd al-Ḥaqq bin Faḍl Ḥaqq al-ʿUmarī. *Sharḥ al-mirqāt.* Edited by ʿAbd al-Ḥamīd al-Turkmānī. ʿAmmān: Dār al-Nūr, 2019.

INDEX OF DEFINITIONS

DETAILED TABLE OF CONTENTS

المُحْتَوَيَاتُ المفصلة

Also from Islamosaic

Ark of Salvation

Connecting to the Quran

Etiquette with the Quran

Infamies of the Soul

Hadith Nomenclature Primers

Hanbali Acts of Worship

Ibn Juzay's Sufic Exegesis

Refutation of Those Who Do Not Follow the Four Schools

Sharḥ Al-Waraqāt

Shaykh al-Sulamī's Waṣiyyah

Supplement for the Seeker of Certitude

The Accessible Conspectus

The Encompassing Epistle

The Evident Memorandum

The Ultimate Conspectus